Stopping the
Gallop to Empire

by CAROL BLY and
CYNTHIA LOVELAND

Bly & Loveland Press
5537 Zenith Avenue South
Edina, MN 55410
loveland@mlecmn.net
www.blyandloveland.com

Library of Congress Control Number: 2004095765
ISBN: 0-9745000-1-1

Front cover photography by
David Trask/Index Stock Imagery

Printed in the United States of America by
Reflections Printing
Minneapolis, MN

Designed by
DeeAnn Hendricks

Set in AGaramond type

Footnotes in *Stopping the Gallop to Empire* appear on the pages of their referent text.
We find it hard to find notes that appear at the end of a book, Chicago style manual
rulings notwithstanding. The original idea behind putting them at the end was to
relieve ambivalent readers of any threatening signs of scholarship on text pages, but
we have noticed that even inexperienced readers are glad to glance at footnoted
material. Further, we have provided quoted passages in closed font so that they can
be located easily. Our general feeling is that the Chicago styles for footnotes, end-
notes, and in-text quotation were not well advised innovations.

Please send all orders and inquiries to
Bly & Loveland Press
5537 Zenith Avenue South
Edina, MN 55410
$15

Table of Contents

Appendix

CHAPTER 1

Galloping in Tryon, North Carolina

In the 1940s, Tryon, North Carolina, was a town with two riding stables. Newman's was used by the Tryon Hunt Club. These were the elite of horsemanship. They organized and ran the steeple chase. At spring break, they and their kids came to Tryon from Boston, New York, Chicago, and Minneapolis, and won most of the prizes at the Tryon Horse Show. The other stable belonged to James Andrews. James's patrons were hacks: that is, they didn't hunt or jump. James owned an assortment of horses and nags. Perhaps most of those animals were decent mounts. I never knew because I was ten years old, untaught, and riddled with fear.

The horse James always backed out for me was Prince, a black beast with a smooth canter. A friend of mine, Helen, always rode Al. We each paid James $2.00 once a week to escort us for an hour's ride. Nearly every week Prince ran away with me before I could stop him. Before James could catch up with him Prince galloped me straight back to the stable, slowing enough thankfully so I could jump before he scraped me off on the nicked lintel.

I was always afraid of Prince, but I kept a brilliantine grin on my face. James clearly disrespected my cowardice. When James looked back to check on us two little girls, I would give him my glassy smile. I gave the horrible, demoralized smile to the African American kids who paused in their clay yards to watch us pass. They touched forelock to James and sometimes said "'Do" to my friend and me. I grinned like a plate at those kids, shouting "Hay!" (Southern for "Hi!") thinking, praying, I would give up my life as a lucky whitefolks' kid and live out my whole life in Black Bottom if only I could be back on the ground with those kids and not up on this terrifying horse.

To get out of town and into the Hunting Country northeast of Tryon, James always led us along a low-slung river road, where the houses were unpainted. The rich, beautiful North Carolina clay made their front yards. People swept them in circle patterns, and set out objects of pride. On the front porches women did family laundry and whitefolks' laundry.

Black Bottom lay along a tributary of the Pacolet River. The road was a sketchy gravel job. Sometimes a car approached. I would try to distract myself from fear by taking an interest in the car, looking to see if it had an A or a C gas ration sticker. So long as we were still in Black Bottom, James led Helen on Al and me on Prince at a walk, or at the most, a slow trot. I gave brilliantine smiles to the few motorists, brilliantine smiles to the kids in their yards. I tried to look friendly and competent. I was nearly always terrified. Soon Prince would run away with me. Life seemed relentless. I knew those little black kids we passed had a microscopic chance of ever being anything you could call "privileged." I knew that I had a microscopic chance of conquering my fear of Prince.

Once Helen had a cold and couldn't ride. My aunt, who could spot cowardice at 17 miles, sent me off to Andrews's stable. James asked where Helen was. I explained, and he didn't even answer. He yanked on his horse's girth, mounted, and off we went.

"That Helen!" he called back to me over his shoulder. "She's got pluck."

And a moment later he said, "This time you must show Prince who's boss." James had told me that a dozen times.

I had already shown Prince who was boss. That horse and I were in perfect agreement. Prince was boss. At whatever moment he chose he would tongue the bit forward from its correct back position in his mouth. When he had it firmly between his upper and lower teeth, he executed a snappy u-ey and took off for the stable barn.

Prince taught me a useful lesson about terror. Whatever doom is coming down on you, it will always feel too late to reverse. By the time I felt that fourth-rate gelding's huge body hardening under me, and he had done his about-face, before he'd begun the gallop back to the barn it felt too late. What I had feared a moment ago had happened, as it would. The familiar landscape suddenly tore up into ragged flashing of sun and shadow and local dogs barking and the faces of bystanders. Those of you who are not afraid of horses, please know this: no bystanders, not even back in the 1940s when bystanders were not the millions and billions of passive people they are now, ever—please know this—no bystanders ever leap over the boxwood hedges and slab fencing to grab your runaway by a rein to save you. They don't do it.

The first thing terror does, I learned from that sub-moral horse Prince, is make whatever is happening seem hopeless. Yet it wasn't hopeless. Even a ten-year-old coward can occasionally stop a runaway stable hack. There is psychological work to do.

First, the rider must make the conscious decision not to fall off and not to get run away with. Next, the rider must curse the horse openly. No more simply begging, "Please, Prince, please, I never beat you, Prince, please, I never beat you! Please stop stop stop!" The horse hears that yellow cry and his heart swells with the pure fun of galloping off, whether away God knows where or simply back to the unpainted stable. The fun of bullying a member of homo sapiens has raised the beast into a glory. (Incidentally, Prince's gallop, as well as his mere canter, was a sail of a smooth ride.) Life can be boring to a gelding with so little love life and no intellectual life. Violence, glorious violence, pounding away down the packed road, bit in one's teeth, is not boring.

I learned I could sometimes, not always, stop Prince. I learned to see-saw the reins so they left his teeth and the bit pulled back savagely at the corners of his mouth. He would stop his gallop. I was afraid he wouldn't like me any more now that I had stopped his gallop. Wouldn't like me! Wouldn't like me! As though it were a question of winning respect by giving way to Prince's own misbehavior!

I would always be afraid of horses. As the neurologists say, those are emotions. You can't do anything about emotions. It is only feelings that you can do something about. Neurologists make a great point of distinguishing between mere physical emotions generated in the body and lower nuclei of the brain and the upper feelings put together by our cortex. Emotions come crowding up into your brain by various means, blood and neurotransmitters to flare up in your amygdala and cingulate. But feelings belong to your soul, so to speak, because they are made up not just of primal consciousness but of previous memories and values and decisions that you, being a particular single organism, have already made. They are yours. All that gassy wordage means is that once we see or hear or touch something, the conscious circuitry which races around, back and forth, checking for previous opinions, checking for this moment's opinions, even rechecking the original input from outside—all that electric cloud of millions of neuron firings in nanoseconds in the cortex—gives you final judgments in whatever the case, wise or unwise—your essential feelings about it.

Well, but we are slow learners. At least I am. Decades went by before I realized that when anything terrifying happens it will seem to be already too late to do anything about it. I had read Pastor Niemoeller's anguished confession that he had been far too slow to stand up against Hitler, but not until 2003 did I connect the feeling of its already being too late to stop Prince with its already being or not being too late to stop, for example, my country from turning into an empire.

The advantage that runaways of any kind, horses or government leaders, have over timorous people is that they always somehow send us the message that it is too late. Too late! Too late! The plans are already made! They seem to say. This is already a police state! Very scary! Last year the United States Treasury Department, for some reason acting on behalf of the Administration, told PEN, the international writers' and readers' association, that PEN was no longer allowed to publish new editions and translations of mid-eastern literature without checking first with the United States government. Terrifying! PEN, however, not being hapless ten-year-olds on horseback, and having read history of totalitarian nations, responded, Oh, is that right? You are having the gall to say that we may not correct previous editions and republish poetry in translation from the Arabic? They made other remarks. The Administration withdrew its proposed censorship over PEN. The trouble is, millions of Americans could have read about the censorship and PEN's statement of ethical outrage about it, but not read the later news which was that the Administration had to rescind that piece of gratuitous bullying and unconstitutionality.[1]

It takes fortitude to stand up for a cause you may lose. Joseph Conrad wrote that a good many people are willing to die fighting for a good cause but that fewer people are willing to continue fighting for a cause that might likely fail.

> "A certain readiness to perish is not so very rare, but it is seldom that you meet men whose souls, steeled in the impenetrable armor of resolution, are ready to fight a losing battle to the last. Which of us here has not observed this, or maybe experienced something of that feeling in his own person this extreme weariness of emotions, the vanity of effort, the yearning for rest? Those striving with unreasonable forces know it well,— the shipwrecked castaways in boats, wanderers lost in a desert, men battling against the unthinking might of nature, or the stupid brutality of crowds."[2]

That is, they are willing to die in their boots, so to speak, but not if the whole enterprise looks hopeless. Standing up in an ambiance of hopelessness, then, takes more guts than joining with millions who expect to win.

We two authors of this book professionally deal with hopelessness in our work. Cynthia is a school social worker. I am a teacher of creative writing. School social work is an ongoing engagement against bad forces in kids' lives. Not only will the worker's success in bracing up a kid show up only later but all the while more victims of family or cultural abuse keep being sent to the worker's office. And as for hopelessness as a stumbling block in the teaching of creative writing, the first thing teacher and want-to-become writer face together is that writer's unconscious decision made piece by piece long ago and over years out of all the gravel of psychological trash thrown by some

---

[1] Sources: Adam Liptak, "Treasury Department is Warning Publishers of the Perils of Criminal Editing of the Enemy." *The New York Times,* February 28, 2004. On April 5, 2004 *The New York Times* ran an article called "Ban is Eased on Editing Foreign Work." Persons who objected strenuously include Joel Conarroe, President of PEN, and counsel for the Institute of Electrical and Electronics Engineers, an international group. PEN's own website provides further coverage on this bizarre attack on freedom of the press.
[2] Joseph Conrad, in *Lord Jim.*.

human beings into the minds of other human beings: What does that psychological trash say? It grins. It says, "Who do you think you are to become a spokesperson for any cause?"

In a practical sense, any ethical foray always is too late. The criminal intentions of cruel leaders are in place and being exquisitely strategized well before the victims—ordinary people—are even thinking of such things. I had ambled along with the slack leafy, autumnal idealism so common to the children of liberals: I looked into the faces of little kids in Black Bottom and supposed as how the United States really ought to do better by them. That was a good 28 years before the Civil Rights movement got to "doing better" by black kids and adults. My family weren't part of doing better by anyone. We gravely disdained Southern whites' behavior towards black people.

I ambled along considering now and then various cruelties practiced on black people the way a fool picks up and glances at things out of someone else's in-box. I didn't distinguish the difference in quality between concepts to do with fairness and the conventions of long division, fractions and decimals. I supposed deep ideas would come my way. They came to Thomas Jefferson. They would come to me. Learning and life would no doubt come along my way. Schoolchildren jog along at a pleasant tempo, like riders with the sun on their arms and most of the branches overhead high enough so you needn't duck.

So Evil always has a head start. Machiavelli explained that if you are planning to overcome a peaceful neighbor and steal everything he's got, you should take advantage of your head start. Do all unlawful invasions quickly. Let the victims feel it's over before they were gathered enough to oppose you.

Average citizens don't get told the two psychological steps to take in order to protect their land: first, decide consciously to oppose the evil. This may sound stupid. A lot of people, however, don't particularly oppose any evil. They sometimes take satisfaction in jeering at the word "evil."

An aside about the word "evil." I think we should hang onto the word. The Christian Coalition people use it freely but language is free for everyone's use. If such language seems extreme all we have to do is remind ourselves, "Is slavery evil or not? Is

shaving hours of overtime pay from workers evil or not? Is torturing military prisoners evil or not? Evil is a useful word, unless
one's own psychological need is for neutral feelings.

Relaxed, inactive citizens may not even precisely "enable"
wrongdoing, to use the language of co-dependence. They don't
oppose it, however, and when confronted about that they show
some handy defenses. In Chapter 7 we offer a list of remarks frequently made by those ethically confronted and some replies that
sometimes work.

The second psychological step is to decide to go on opposing
the evil even when it feels or actually is too late (the difficulty
Conrad mentioned). Thomas Paine, on a slightly different but
related aspect of this subject, pointed out that if an evil is new
enough it may not even seem like an ethical issue at all. The vast
lot of Europeans and Americans didn't really understand how serious an issue was the individual rights of man. They were rather
sleepy about it. If Paine had been in the 1980s women's movement he'd have said, "Well, they just aren't getting it." Not seeing
evil for what it is is a classical psychological habit of citizens
which sidetracks or delays their own proper indignation. Paine
paid attention to citizens who, being morally so sleepy and casual, have a stronger taste for neutral opinions or no opinions than
for uncomfortable opinions.

> "Perhaps the sentiments contained in the following
> pages are not yet sufficiently fashionable to procure
> general favor; a long habit of not thinking a thing
> wrong gives it a superficial appearance of being right,
> and raises at first a formidable outcry in defense of cus-
> tom. But the tumult soon subsides. Time makes more
> converts than reason."[3]

Here is a reality check about courage in a hopeless situation:
sometimes one can stop a powerful horse and sometimes not. I
knew how to see-saw the reins in Prince's mouth. Sometimes I

---

[3] Thomas Paine, in *Common Sense, The Rights of Man and Other Essential Writing of Thomas
Paine*, 1984 Penguin, A Meridian Book with an introduction by Sidney Hook, New American
Library, page 23 of Common Sense.

managed it. At other times he all but scraped me off the saddle by galloping under the barn door. Once Hitler was in power many, many groups, especially of young people opposed the Nazis with publications and by smuggling Jews out over the borders at night. Many were caught. Their secret presses were found. Nazi custom was to guillotine the editors. In the months after 1933 Germany's borders got tighter and tighter. Here are two essential points about those Germans who opposed the Third Reich when it looked too late and even when it was too late: some decided to do it anyway. The people whose lives they managed to save got to live the rest of their lives. Some of them wrote grateful books about it. So when we say such and such an effort is too little or too late, it's historically useful to be clear about too late for the rescuers and too late for those rescued is not always the same thing.

As we offer a book called *Stopping the Gallop to Empire*, we know perfectly well that the United States could lose the battle to keep itself a republic. The present administration might win four years' more power in November of 2004. Such a win would be tremendously exhilarating for those who want this country for their own empire. It is ridiculous of liberals to shriek, "How could anyone want to etc., etc.!" It helps to pretend you are an empire-wanter. For example, the Romans loved having an empire. John Rawls[4] may judge a nation by how it treats its least powerful citizens, but that isn't how most of us feel most of the time. Everyday life is what moves us. The Romans were delighted when their expansion to southern Italy brought them into armed conflict with the Greek colonists there and in Sicily. The Greeks were and are marvelous cooks. The Romans developed a mania for ethnic food. They brought in Greek slaves for a lot of domestic work and school tutoring, of course, but also to cook. They were crazy about ethnic foods from others of their Occupied Countries. Life is gorgeous in an empire if you're in a position to make use of it. And everywhere he went doors opened to a Roman free man because he could say "Civis romanus sum."

However, if conservatives are formally educated and not in

---

[4] John Rawls is the Harvard philosophy professor with several books of fascinating insights into, among much else, public morals.

the habit of ignoring injustices where they show up, comfy empire life does not assuage their unease. Their anxiety may come and go, but it is there, moving like a viscous subsurface aquifer in human brains. Conservatives haven't all got a taste for tyranny. Even if up to the present they have gone along with what is called neo-conservatism, now they are restive and frustrated.

High-minded conservatives like high-minded anyone else have the unequivocal habit of sorting their lives into priorities. Serving the Friends of the Symphony is good. Beauty is good. Disfunding public schools is bad. Making USA classrooms so huge that one can't learn to think in them is bad. Let's say that thousands of civilized people are having to juggle those two goals, aesthetic culture and public education. What if civilized people thus worried make up 55% of the conservatives in the United States?

Our thoughts are for them.

A one-time swing vote on November 2nd by the population for whom this book is written would be enough voters to cleanly save democracy for another four years at least.
Inside such people there often lives a half-conscious idealism.

A seriously idealistic (principled) conservative is someone who is not simply voting his or her portfolio or corporate position dependent upon the good will of a neo-conservative administration. He or she may, of course, be surrounded in the gated psychology of the rich. It is dangerously blithe of liberals to pronounce all conservatives either self-interested predators or riders on a gravy train. It's a wrong take on conservatives. Thousands and tens of thousands of Republicans who are gorgeously educated, many of whom, for example, have even read and even remember what's in the Constitution, still tend to cling to the coastline of their old Party affiliation. A sailor needn't know any principles of navigation if he plies along the shoreline. A citizen needn't trust and apply any ethical moral idea into his or her life if he or she plies near enough the old cant.

Thomas Paine ruefully noticed how hard it is to stand alone. Writing about the Colonies' break with England, he said colonists who did not want to break with England consisted of four kinds:

> "Interested men, who are not to be trusted; weak
> men, who cannot see; prejudiced men, who will not
> see, and (he added) a certain class of moderate men,
> who think better of the European world than it
> deserves; and this last class, by an ill-judged delibera-
> tion, will be the cause of more calamities to this conti-
> nent, than all the other three."[5]

We are writing to present-day conservatives who want to think
better of the present administration than it deserves. Breaking
with one's own loyalties and thinking badly of one's associates
are ravaging to any civil person's peace of mind. You feel your
own confidence in your own ethics under assault somehow.
Psychologically fragile people, especially fragile people with a
tendency to social climbing, have the hardest time because they
so much like the communal spirit of being with others, especially
others whom they respect a good deal. They typically use a common phrase that rather lets the cat out of the bag: "I have made
my peace with" (such and such an organization).

That phrase is so gracious, it is so handsome! And in its por-
tentous way it sounds spirited. It is a kind of ethical Freudian slip,
however. If we have "made our peace with an organization," it
means we have decided to no longer hold it to certain standards
that we once held it to. Putting the best face on it, we intend to
be tolerant. A less attractive interpretation is that having been
unable to lick 'em we have decided to join 'em. I most commonly
have heard that expression used by doctrinal unbelievers who
attend a church for its music and high-minded camaraderie. They
explain, not cynically, but with a total lack of psychological
awareness, that "they have made their peace with that church."
Their idea is that the beauty of the liturgy and the general kindli-
ness of the congregation make up for the embarrassment of lying
one's way through the creeds.

No one will unkindly ask that churchgoer, "So then—you

---

[5] Thomas Paine, *Common Sense*, page 41.

have decided to give the church your aid and comfort?" (The reference is "giving aid and comfort to the enemy," a classic definition of treason.) No one would be so intrusive or stupid, especially in this country which protects separation of church and state. Besides, if churches filled to 100% with hypocrites no harm done provided we keep that wall between church and state. Hypocrites don't necessarily hurt one another and in my experience they don't go witch-hunting after non-church members either.

But in things to do with the *res publica*, or well being of the republic, it matters tremendously if liberals or conservatives, either one, are casually voting for their respective parties because they "have made peace with them"—that is, basically having thrown in the moral towel and no longer caring much what their party does.

American history doesn't stop on November 2nd, 2004. Young people now regarding us adults with that jaunty, half-morbid, half-admiring curiosity that young people treat their elders to will be watching to see how many of our principles we actually stand for. They will notice if we "make peace with some organization" that our own hearts shouldn't logically be making peace with. Some of them will be cynical about it. "That's life in the real world, I suppose," they will say. They may be courteous good sports about it when they find their parents to be voting without principles. Being a good sport doesn't mean having a glad heart, though.

If they are rebellious young people they will decide, privately, one hopes—not humiliating us to our faces—that we have sold out and in their time they are certainly going to do things differently.

CHAPTER 2

Whom is this book for and why?

I t is for lucky (which means educated) people of a conservative cast of mind who now feel grave and uneasy on behalf of the United States.

But why ever, for the love of heaven, would a book called *Stopping the Gallop to Empire* be for those people? Why isn't our book for people who are much scarier? This book is for those educated, anxious conservatives because when all arguments are made and images of cruel or terrifying outcomes are fully laid before us all, those who will best rebuild our already financially despoiled and half-smashed infrastructure will be idealistic, principled, lucky (for which read well-educated) people with enough will and leisure to drive themselves, not only on November 2, 2004, but afterward.

For the sake of clarity, but briefly: whom is this book *not* for?

It is not for fundamentalist Christians or fundamentalist economists because they want merciful government for themselves but not for everyone.

It is not for people stuck in psychological development stage 2—i.e., whose highest ideals are tribal and family loyalty.

It is not for Americans, either liberal or conservative, whose vote is only self-serving—that is, not for Republicans who vote their portfolio or who need to demonstrate to higher-up party members that they are loyal and therefore should benefit when plums are being sent around.

It is not for Democrats who vote Democratic only because they are union-affiliated and are told to vote Democratic.

It is not for third-party voters who naively want to feel good, rather pure, like Boy and Girl Scouts, about their vote, and it is not for USA single-issue voters who vote for whichever party has a platform corner that promises protection for a particular hobby interest, such as carrying a concealed weapon.

It is not for social climbers because social climbing is a major passion that steers people's ethics without their noticing it.

Finally, it is not for people who are emotionally drawn to war. They do not even begin to imagine what war is really like.

When we teach a little kid to swim, we take into account at every second how uncertain this feels to the child, what a shock water is, how to a child danger lurks in the horrifying image of depths the way monsters lurk in one's dark bedroom at night. Some children take to water easily. A lot don't. We caretakers and swimming instructors acknowledge, and what's more, respect the child's anxiety. We don't hesitate to help. We remind little kids how much more confident and competent they are today than yesterday.

"Yes but it's scary!" they say. And we say, "You bet it is! And you are smart to be scared. It's hard to get the right balance of smart caution and glorious adventurousness going right! It's hard!"

We don't pretend to children that learning to leave their own milieu, air, in order to be playful and competent in such a very different milieu, water, has no psychological dynamics to it. We openly talk with kids about the psychological property called being afraid. They pick up from us that psychological dynamics are for real. Well, and what's the good of making psychological dynamics real? This: once one invisible dynamic is real to you and respectable because adult mentors give it a name aloud you make a cognitive jump: you now are open to feeling—on your own— the reality of other invisible dynamics. One of these invisible dynamics is a human being's will power.[1]

Children set their will power the better for hearing an adult talk about the funny mix of invisible stuff involved in learning to swim—curiosity, fear, pride in competence.

If there is one field of inquiry that exasperates otherwise-educated rich people it is conversations about psychological dynamics. Note: privileged people don't seem to mind psychiatry. In fact, on the East coast they pay for much of it. That is not so surprising because psychiatry is about as ethics-neutral as any professional field. For starters, it is a valuable for-sale treatment of personal needs—treatment for a huge range of grief from personal stress to mental illness. But the idea of certain psychological dynamics working in normal people—working in all of us including normal privileged people is anathema to otherwise educated people. They have an impressive vocabulary of pejorative labels on the subject. In the 1970s, "psychobabble." In the 1980s "psychobabble" and "psychological slush-funding" and "permissive drivel." In the 1990s and 2000s all three: "psychobabble," "psychological slush-funding," and "permissive drivel."

As to decision-making in the public sphere, otherwise-educated people of privilege discount the psychological aspects of domestic economic policy making and foreign policy making. The great graduate schools of government and business pay cursory attention. Even the Harvard Business School, which has some marvelous coursework on human behavior as shown and/or discussed in literature, has nothing about 1990s insights into the psychology of ethics.[2]

One of the most fascinating remarks that therapists make is "It is time that you were afraid. It's a good thing, not a bad thing."

There aren't enough teachers in our culture to tell everyone, "You need to learn to feel afraid! You should be afraid!" Smart senators and smart, even conservative, journalists and cultural critics beg the privileged to be afraid of losing the United States to empire. In September, 2004, it is hard to guess how much critical mass that canny advice has.[3] Thomas Jefferson wrote openly that he was afraid of losing republics to empire because most people are so ignorant and anxious to hide in their private lives that they won't vote carefully. (Jefferson thought *he* knew about people not bothering to vote!)

---

[1] Especially see Antonio Damasio in *Looking for Spinoza*, about how not everything in the brain is determined, not by any means, and Spinoza the ethicist could be called the first psychologist. On page 274, for example, Damasio describes a part of Spinoza's moral message and following it, on page 275 writes: "Spinoza's solution hinges on the mind's power over the emotional process…" We find "the mind's power over the emotional process" a handsome phrase for free will.

[2] This statement is from our investigations into Harvard, Stanford, Wharton and eight other graduate schools of business administration during 2003. Our work may already be out of date.

[3] We are so grateful and impressed by the outcries of Senator Edward Kennedy and the conservative journalist Charley Reese in *The Orlando Sentinel* and in two speeches of George Soros. Any one of these substantial people, each of whom has a career of good fight behind them, could have decided the hell with getting into this critical fray, but they didn't.

In chapter 5 on neurology we discuss how the more a brain is taught to contemplate and imagine, the more altruism it is capable of. That's a simple idea: of course someone who is willing to imagine another person's situation can make out objects the way that other person makes out objects. One might want to help. One might want to give that other person a less tippy playfield. One might.

What is so interesting in the last two decades of the 20th and this first decade of the 21st century is that neuroscience seems now to be confirming that the mid-20th century moral stage developmentalists had been right all along. That is, the brain is programmed for the potential of getting more and more subtle *and altruistic* in its thinking. We must scrupulously note the difference between the brain's being programmed to perform in such and such a way and the brain's being programmed for the *potential* of performing in such and such a way. Genes specify much, but very, very little compared to how a brain becomes as it goes.[4]

That's a very ethics-loaded concept. That ethics-loaded concept is getting more and more validation from the brain sciences.

Well—wonderful! But not wonderful if you have all your life been loyal to a we slash they philosophy that says we are entitled to wash our hands of the they's.

Most conservatives don't know enough psychology even to be afraid of how the brain yearns for a unified philosophy with some ethical elegance to it. Their resistance to respecting and looking into psychological dynamics would not seem to come from fear that if they became conscious of a handsome philosophy growing in themselves they would feel constrained to give up avarice, to give up milking the government of its moneys heretofore designed for the many, and so forth. More likely they despise psychology because everyone they know despises social psychology. We need something that is OK for open jeering. For them psychology fills the bill. Another factor in their disrespect for psychology is that jeering is pure attitude: that is, you needn't do any

[4] Please see Matt Ridley's accessible discussion of genes in *Genome: The Autobiography of a Species in 23* Chapters. New York, HarperCollins, 2000. We have not yet read his new book, *Nature via Nurture: Genes, Experience, and What Makes Us Human.* New York, HarperCollins, 2003.

thinking in order to jeer. All you have to do is listen around and see what attractive people of your acquaintance are jeering at— and join them.

Whereas, the moment one begins asking the kind of questions that ethical wakening in the brain makes one ask one begins to think. And then, fascinating as the thinking may be, a quiver of fear gets in, silvery as a snake, from some depths of one's mind. Those who have the habits of intellectual life don't mind that fear because it is a small price to pay for the break from life's dumb conversations. But very privileged persons may not have the intellectual habit, so they venture a half-inch into asking themselves psychological questions, feel the fear—and straightaway back out. Their usual mindset says, "Sir, Madam, you are entitled not to have fearful thoughts." Their usual mindset adds, "Sir, Madam, weren't you and your spouse just talking about looking into that Ellesmere Island tour, where they have that informed, but laid back non-snotty naturalist explaining the bird life, what's wrong with you guys signing on before it slips your mind?" The mindset is practicing a dysfunctional but powerful response to fear called *distraction*.

Liberals just in themselves can be a block to conservatives' learning to be philosophical. Liberals shriek and blame, or if their manners are better than that, they generally make it clear they are better than you are—and what's more, they've been better, more ethical, than you, ever since graduation. In fact, both liberals and conservatives need to leave off making all the cheap shots.

Getting smart about psychological dynamics means sacrificing some of the delicious attitudinal stuff. Democrats would have to sacrifice their moral condescension at the very sound of rightist talk…"I just can't understand how they can think that…..etc. etc." Such outrage or calm head-shaking, and the range between, is tremendously satisfying. Liberals absolutely know they are better people than conservatives. They may say, "O well, but we all have our own opinions, etc." but they are posing because they feel they are more right-minded than conservatives. No one pays a Democrat to do political heeling, whereas oddly deep pools of money show up for Republicans who pull off certain political tasks. They or their friends get defense contracts. They or their friends get on decision-making committees which have say in the fate of American public schools. Of course liberals feel superior.

And conservatives take nourishment and satisfaction with all their being from the idea that some truths are stable forever. Sad truths sometimes, but at least they stay put. "The poor are always with us"—a line that is the peak of any glacial rhetoric floating huge and cold. Such sturdy tenets as "Look, the poor will always be poor" and "There will always be wars" relieve everyone of any critical mass of sorrow about the poor or dead eighteen-year-olds. It shouldn't surprise anyone that few conservatives take seriously any scholarship so unshipshape as the study of normal psychological dynamics. Chekhov saw how comfortable one can be no matter how appalling other people's circumstances:

"...I said to myself: how many contented, happy people there really are! What an overwhelming force they are! Look at life: the insolence and idealness of the strong, the ignorance and brutishness of the weak, horrible poverty everywhere, overcrowding, degeneration, drunkenness, hypocrisy, lying. Yet in all the houses and on all the streets there is peace and quiet; of the fifty thousand people who live in our town there is not one would cry out, not one who would vent his indignation aloud. We see the people who go to market, eat by day, sleep by night, who babble nonsense, marry, grow old, good-naturedly drag their dead to the cemetery, but we do not see or hear those who suffer, and what is terrible in life goes on somewhere behind the scenes. Everything is peaceful and quiet and only mute statistic protest: so many people gone out of their minds, so many gallons of vodka drunk, so many children dead from malnutrition— and such a state of things is evidently necessary; obviously the happy man is at ease only because the unhappy ones bear their burdens in silence, and if there were not this silence, happiness would be impossible. It is a general hypnosis. Behind the door of every contented, happy man their ought to be someone standing with a little hammer and continually reminding him with a knock that there are unhappy people, that however happy he may be, life will sooner or later show him its claws, and trouble will come to him—illness, poverty, losses, and then no one will see or hear him, just as now he neither sees nor hears others. But there is no man with a hammer. The happy man lives at his ease, faintly fluttered by small daily cares, like an aspen in the wind—and all is well."[5]

Our interest in this book is centered on the psychological approach to citizenship because psychology sets out to underscore for us those of our feelings that are less comfy than other feelings we have. As for the feelings stirred up in citizenship, our public life, or our lack of public life if we have tidily kept ourselves out of it so far, carries with it two kinds of alarm.

The first is anxiety over what our government makes happen or threatens to make happen soon. The second is our having to act tolerant toward fellow-citizens.

Both of these feelings are part of fear. Until a few weeks ago I thought of myself in these ways: I was someone who felt nearly constant anxiety about the present United States government, but who meanwhile, back at the ranch, so to speak, had a merely neighborly attitude towards strangers I saw.

One hot Minneapolis morning, I took a two-year-old grandson to the public water park. He let himself eagerly over the wading-pool edge in his trusty diaper-trunks. He jumped and splashed. With his tiny arms he pretended to do the crawl. He'd seen bigger boys and girls crawl. I watched, dangling my legs over the pool edge in my sopped jeans. Next thing, a cheerful, noisy crowd of much bigger kids leapt into the other end of the pool. They soon splashed and dunked and pretended to drown one another all over the pool. None of these kids ever got near my grandson, and two of them gave me friendly grins as they went careening by for all the world like creature-ships out of Jules Verne.

Suddenly I decided they were old enough already to have absorbed between four and ten years of USA television watching

---

[5] Anton Chekhov, from the short story "Gooseberries."

and might be prone to violence. The seven or eight of them now seemed legion. It might occur to them to drown or at least terrify a much smaller little boy for the fun of it. Since people over twenty like Pfc. Lynndie England and Specialist Sabrina Harman and Megan Ambuhl could declare they tortured their Iraqi prisoners just for the fun of it,[6] it was no big deal, and so forth, why wouldn't these much younger people be still more unconstrained in what they chose to do just for fun?

I kept on returning the big kids' smiles for two reasons. First, they were friendly kids. Second, I had quickly finished my plan for the Worst Case. I would grab one or more of them by the throat if they threatened Teddy. Once I had that unpleasant plan in place, I didn't have to stay conscious of it. I could enjoy the wading pool population. I was happy that strangers could still use public facilities together in America. The wading pool was not gated. I am a liberal arts graduate of the old kind. I have the old liberal-arts longing to treat all people civilly until they prove themselves dangerous. I felt that civil tolerance of others that gets taught K through 12 and 13 through 16 to those who get to study history of other lands than ours and read Richard Wright and Richard Leakey on which species was the real cause of the last extinction on earth.

Still, I noticed I had quietly slid off the pool edge and begun wading around near to my grandson. I was not so afraid of those bigger children as I am of the current government. I was afraid, however. Any level of fear is unpleasant. If no one had advised you K through 16 to have some sort of "liberal stance" about unlike enclaves of the populace you would be free to do what privileged people have done ever since Neolithic society changed to Early Civilization society: stay clear. In what is called "Early Civilization," the privileged scrupulously designed the town so the rich got some distance from the very poor.

We have no written history to tell us why the early town-planners wanted distance from the poor. Nowadays whatever the level

---

[6] Refer to the NY Times coverage. Also available online is the text of Barbara Ehrenreich's Commencement Address to the Barnard class of 2004 in which she said she had meant to do an address on the cost of higher education but now wanted to speak about U.S. Army women's torturing of Iraqi prisoners. Ehrenreich got off a great rouser: "The uterus is no substitute for a conscience."

of privilege of the lucky they want distance from the desperately poor for one practical reason and one psychological reason. You want to be able to carry in two or three bags of groceries and then return for the remainder without finding that someone has removed the car battery, the CD player, and a wheel. The psychological reason is that one feels, as group facilitators would say, 'uncomfortable' around the very poor because all poverty is cruel and unnecessary. No one should be very poor. It's cruel! Even educated people had rather have no feeling or nearly neutral feeling much of time than live with background guilt. If you distract yourself from your non-neutral feelings such as shame that people are poor by picking up the remote, most people do it. For example, say that you happen to remember what happened as a result of then-Governor Ronald Reagan getting his Proposition 13 through the California legislature.[7] Mental patients were turned out of institutions into the streets and supports to the poor were slashed. Horrible to think of. Still, look, here is a stunner of a funeral to watch. You can forget the man and watch the expensive rite. Actually one can distract oneself from nearly anything by plunging into tears at a funeral. If they play and sing the Navy hymn it hardly matters whose funeral it is because the lines and the melody of that hymn are so beautiful. Even if explorers and merchant sailors and Navy personnel have never had any evidence that God "is strong to save" and "bids the mighty ocean its own appointed place to keep," the hymn is unmistakably beautiful. All wishful dreams are beautiful. In any case, distraction by rich celebration, or as mentioned earlier by turning one's thoughts to a well-earned vacation, or by any other means, is identified by the field of social work as one of the most classical ways to ward off painful thinking.

We keep saying who our audience is: conservatives, let us suppose with incomes between $80,000 and $8,000,000 p.a.

---

[7] Proposition 13 was a referendum (called "ballot initiative") voted into law in California in 1978. It gloriously reduced property tax rates by an average of 57%. It is now regarded as presaging taxpayer revolt throughout the United States. In 2003 Governor Schwarzenegger clamped down on advisor Warren Buffett's suggestion they remove Proposition 13. A point of interest: The United States Constitution does not provide for ballot initiatives under which proposed legislation can be submitted for direct voting at the polls. See http://www.fact-index.com/c/california.

$80,000 is enough to allay day-to-day fears and to avoid dressing like the medium-poor. $8,000,000 is as high as the authors of this book can imagine. (In truth we really can't imagine $8,000,000 but we thought we had better put it in because lots of conservatives and liberals both do have that much, before bonuses even.) In addition to the $80,000 minimum, let's say our conservatives were lucky enough to be educated in the liberal arts. The liberal arts (this tiresome label that we keep mentioning because it is vital) leads its lucky protégés to a taste for history, literature, math, and foreign languages. Those four subjects depend upon and get their glory from *concept*. Concept, and the abstract thinking it takes, along with experience to get to it.

Concept, roughly speaking, is the generalizations one makes as soon as one sees a pattern between one event or place and any other. An example that little kids learn: you have 3 potted trees and 24 bareroot seedling trees. You learn how to plant them. That's just science fair stuff. You have 27 trees. As long as you realize only that three trees plus twenty-four trees makes twenty-seven trees you still haven't a concept. When the teacher, however, then says, three of anything plus twenty-four of that same thing makes twenty-seven of that thing no matter what the things and no matter where it is and in no matter what language you use to hear this, that is a universal concept. Dull to adults, but for little kids it lets the mind sail out of the pale harbor of mere anecdote and mere personalities into the big imaginative sea of things.

Why is concept such a pleasure to the mind? A guess: the mind knows that concept is eternal. The three potted trees and the twenty-four bare-root planted trees will live and die, but the idea of addition is eternal. Well, so what? For intellectuals eternal rules of math or science or any other carefully built, respectable, and replicable theories are gratifying because the mind likes to rearrange concepts and build new theories across the old ones. Yet those of us who love eternal truths aren't all intellectuals.

Here is another guess then. So far as we know homo sapiens is the only creature that contemplates itself. We alone observe ourselves thinking and feeling, so we have got it together in our heads whether we like it or not that we, like the other animals, are going to experience death. We have that unpleasant insight only because some of our thinking process makes an image of ourselves. Socrates has convinced us that "the unexamined life isn't worth living" all right but we could do without that part of the examining that shows us our own upcoming deaths. Remember how Scrooge did not want to look down into the grave that the Ghost of Christmas Yet To Come pointed to. With all his heart Scrooge did not want to look at it.

Likely the undyingness of concepts, then, cheers us up. Let's try an old eighth-grade logical trick for testing the truth of a geometric theorem. Let us suppose that we are not who we are and see if it casts any light.

Let's pretend for a moment that we are not homo sapiens. That is, let's empathize with the others. We are easy slow-grazing wildebeests and gazelles. We have caught sight of two or three lionesses who have successfully vetted our part of the veldt. Now they have plumped themselves down, pushing and growling, to yank out the softer parts of a friend of ours. We can't clearly recall the friend. In fact, maybe it was one of the kids. Maybe some other lady's kid. Our recall is getting fuzzy. Everything is a little neutral. Even the liquid ruby noses and jaws of the lionesses over there—they are a little neutral. We never have had much to do with lions actually. Mom mentioned them, I think it was Mom. Someone in our herd did. Whatever. Anyway. We twist our necks idly to watch from a distance, quietly. Here is a little low place, still moist, with more beautiful yellow grass. It is still pungent to the nose. Tremendously nice.

To the grazing animal, lions are not an enemy to be planned for well in advance. They are not particularly memorable. Much is not memorable. One's herd colleagues being eaten…speaking of being eaten, thank goodness we gazelles have hooves so lions make a point of killing rather than just chewing on in from wherever they caught hold lest our hooves break their jaws—two new lionesses now sprawled on a rise, nearer—nearer this low place where the grass is sweeter—everything is a landscape or some landscape event, like lightning or a smart rainfall on the few trees, on the yellow grass. I am going back to grazing because this grass was given to us and we have a right to graze peacefully on it.

If instead of "going back to grazing even though still within sight of the lionesses" you read "get on with my own life" it may be a parallel for people totally excluded from the disciplines that show you how to be seriously conscious of other.

There is a huge difference between those hundreds of thousands of Republicans who feel so indignant and worried today and those for whom anything outside of their own life, which they feel they have a right to get on with—governments, public ethics, constitutionality—is not much felt. Hundreds of thousands of uneasy Republicans is not many in a nation of between two hundred and three hundred million people. Why focus on them?

Those anxious conservatives are enough to save our republic—whether they get it done before the November, 2004, elections or with greater difficulty, later. There are enough serious conservative idealists to save American decency.

CHAPTER 3

Quickly—psychologically speaking only— what are people's various feelings as a democracy seems to be teetering into an empire?

We can get all the news and read all the history we can bear about republics in danger of being toppled by a few people at the top. This chapter is not about such facts, but about a very few of the psychological dynamics involved.

What do people want from a government anyhow? Actually we don't think about that very much, which doesn't mean it isn't a good question to be asking. The right (psychological, inward) questions don't always get asked. An example: thousands of people choose vacation places and activities that they don't want at all. They get into recreational vehicles of one kind or another. They go somewhere to get away from it all. They do not ask, as they stand in the tin upright casket of an RV shower if they want to be in this vehicle. The "it all" that they are getting away from included hours and hours of solitude perhaps. Well, there's no solitude once you get into an RV.

With government then: we could jot a small list of who wants what. Some don't want any government except sufficient police to deter vandals. Some want democracy or republic, both forms of which are unnatural to mammals and must be vigilantly guarded against thieves. Some want a rigid structure because you obey its logical-sounding laws. But it does not invite citizen participation in its inner circles. One thinks of beautiful Switzerland where no one may use a noisy typewriter after ten o'clock in an apartment house. The Swiss have an ugly history with regard to Nazi deposits in their vaults, but if a government is orderly and never drags its people to war, well, there you are, in armchair states- men's language.

In the United States, who wants it to be empire? Thousands profit from its international economics. On the bottom level, thou- sands join its armed services and don't worry themselves about what orders they will be asked to carry out. At least hundreds at the top get tremendous satisfaction from the huge power that America now has. Of course some people set about vandalizing the treasury and other government moneys any how they can work it, but under any form of government there is always someone skillfully trying to lick up the whole structure for themselves.

A good way to understand what other people are about is deliberately to take some time to pretend you are they. Carl von Clausewitz, (1780-1831), an enlisted soldier who rose up through the ranks in the Prussian army, taught in his book called *On War* that you should make a great point of hypothesizing, then checking out, the enemy's psychology. For over a century the Prussians jeered at him. Now Clausewitz is either required or recommended reading for first-year men and women in military academies all over the world.

Question for us now, then, in case we are jeering at the idea of using professional social psychology with respect to public affairs: do we resemble Prussian military autocrats: are we jeering instead of thinking?

About empires: they come naturally. They are the first primitive form of anything past chieftain-and-armed-males trooping around shooting food and smashing up other tribes' settlements. When animals and insects do manage a form of government more sophisticated than chief-and-troops what they have is empire: some one or two of them get and hold the power to make everyone else take orders and conform.

To get a democracy or republic, on the other hand, you need for someone to have the passionate idea of breaking up whatever chief-and-troops structure or empire has been in place in favor of these 2 principles: big families don't get to run everything just because they're big, and two, everyone, even the top people, must live under the law.

Now those two ideas are very unnatural. They are the passionate products of great minds. In nature big things naturally eat little things, or in turn tiny things (viri and bacilli) eat big things. In nature, everything is just a practical problem. In unnatural structures, like democracy where people vote and that makes the law or in republics where people's voted-for delegates vote on legislation, what you have is a government practicing constraint upon itself. The great political inventors have been people with the luck to have had the four greatest blessings to the human brain: leisure and education and freedom from fear and solitude enough to hatch up wonderful ideas. They themselves can say (and have written into history in some cases): here is what a government tends towards if not restrained from piggery. Here is what a government ought to be. It will take constraint and exertion and vigilance against enemies. They always warn us: some of the enemies will be thugs among our own people.

Altruism seems to bring a kind of high with it. We feel it in great political writing of government leaders. There is unmistakable gaiety in Lincoln at his best, for example. It is a mistake cynically to take all political rhetoric as someone being full of himself. In fact, an altruistic leader finds high adventure in designing ways to keep the lucky from clipping and bullying the less lucky—just the way more natural, self-serving men and women find high adventure in clipping and bullying where they can. (They would call it knowing "the real world" and "working the system.") It reminds anyone old enough to have admired Benjamin Spock of how he imagined a two-year-old feeling when you shout "No, no!" from all the way across the room. Dr Spock advised the parent to get near the child. If you call from across the room, the child, Dr Spock said, "asks himself, 'Am I a man or a mouse?'" and keeps on doing whatever the mischief was that he had been doing.

Thus Solon in the very early 6th century B.C. and towards the end of that century, Cleisthenes came forward with unnatural structures to save Greek cities and countryside from constant tribal quarreling. Just to give one example: in Solon's time the family tribes pushed as hard as they could to get power for their own family tribe by fighting and shoving the other Greek tribes. It was always a bracing up of we against they, most of it according to family affiliation. Solon rode over them with his very unnatural concept of everyone being universally under the law. Cleisthenes then broke up the great Greek families' rivalry by designing for Greece legislative groups each one of which consisted of men from the four different areas of Greece. It was an amazing concept. No animal except the contemplative, inquiring, hypothesizing, experimenting human being would come up with any such re-organizational idea.

The natural thing is for the we, whoever has power, to show everyone else our claws. Since an empire is perfectly natural to mammals, its leaders' minds keep a huge psychological distance between we's and they's: an empire's leaders instinctively regulate for themselves and their friends a separate set of feelings for we's, another set of feelings or a dismissal of any major feelings, for they's.

Democracy being a cultural, not natural, construction, its leaders keep making imaginative efforts to somewhat bring the luckies and the less luckies to equal rights.

Why make so much of we/they being natural and we-they-brought-together being unnatural—and therefore civilized and difficult? For starters, it clears the air to make this illuminating inquiry of oneself. We can look back over our day just spent and list everything we did in three columns entitled, respectively:

1. What I did today that was philosophically meaningless but pleasant? Even if nothing to do with my own intrinsic principles why should it be? Who's a saint?
2. What I did today that served only we and bloody why shouldn't it?
3. What I did today that brings we together with they, if anything?

The first column will consist of activities conventionally called Recreation. It is utterly natural to all mammal species. Rich and middle-class and poor, powerful and powerless, spend time in all three columns. The rich, especially those unemployed or half-employed or totally retired, spend noticeable time and income in Column 1. If they are rich with no particular taste for civic ideals they spend considerable time in Column 2, as well. In column 2 belong one's family concerns, family church affiliation. If they are rich and educated to principles they spend some time in Column 3, such as furthering privileges, rights, division of wealth for the they. This is the well known noblesse oblige.

The poor spend as much time as they can in Column 1, too. In Solange De Santis's terrific book[1] about working on the assembly line at GM's Scarbrough, Ontario, plant before it closed down, she described how ingeniously the auto workers fitted up some poker tables out of cardboard boxes reinforced with duct tape. You kept one of these near your work station, so that the moment it was time for the 16-minute break, the players could instantly assemble to play. The desperately poor, who wouldn't get hired by GM at all, also buy fun for whatever exhausted, half-starved leisure hours they win from holding, say, one and a half full-time jobs typically paying $7.50 an hour in 2000.

The most exasperating aspect of democracy is that it requires that one or more leaders restrain some of their own and others' natural selfishness at the same time as they must wish all this governmental virtue on a huge populace who don't know and don't care and what is all the fuss about because—this is the populace speaking—everyone knows people don't do anything except for their own good anyhow. Back when Hillary Clinton was trying to forward a national health scheme for the United States—a perfect democratic ideal, perfectly workable, desperately needed if you count the poor as people who could make some use of medical services—what Hillary had to overcome was not just predictable conservative special-interest opponents but a huge uninterested populace.

How does one arouse anything better than cynicism and disbelief in the very millions who will benefit should an idealistic proposal get made? A lie told people is that self-interest is the only motivation of homo sapiens. This lie isn't always told directly. Here is an instance in which school psychologists, generating a film against shoplifting, indirectly implied to the kids that self-interest is the motivation to take seriously. In the 1970s the public schools ran the film. It explained why you shouldn't shoplift. The reasons given were, first, that theft eventually raised the prices of products on the market since owners who were stolen from would raise their prices to cover the estimated annual losses from thievery. And second, if you were cited for shoplifting, it would prejudice your getting recommended to any of the armed service academies. Those are only circumspect reasons. The real reason not to shoplift is that it is cruel to whomever you steal from.

---

[1] Solange De Santis, *Life on the Line: One Woman's Tale of Work, Sweat, and Survival.* New York : Doubleday, 1972.

The word cruelty was not used anywhere in the film, however. The word cruel, significantly enough, is seldom used by anyone behaving naturally. It is a popular word only with those promoting ideal behavior. It is a popular word with those promoting unnatural, civilized, desirable relations between people and groups of people. Choice of language bears thinking about.

Bearing in mind, then, the phrase we/they and the contrast of natural with unnatural, we can make a list of the hoped-for outcomes of those who want to change a democracy into empire. Let's call these people "empire-wanters."

1. Empire-wanters want to lick off all the cream of the nation's treasury that they can without wrecking the structure so badly that it can't generate future moneys. The ordinary poor will become and remain Desperately Poor, which works out very well because they will work 2 jobs at between $6 and $8 an hour each, just to keep alive. The Desperately Poor will do the scut work. If they do it too long on the meager and unhealthy diet available to them they will begin to fail the work. They can be fired without difficulty because a) they wouldn't have enough money to sue and b) more of the Desperately Poor[2] will take their places.

2. Empire-wanters want to reduce the they of the empire to a low level of education in conceptual thinking—in the liberal arts and basic sciences—without wrecking the they's ability to do basically slave labor. That is, to atrophy people's development of elegant thinking pathways in the cortex, while kitting out the people technically well enough for bottom-level jobs. The privileged leaders' children will attend, as they do now, traditional private schools with the classical values. In the wonderfully small classes the kids learn to discuss issues openly with confidence. They learn to write argument with brisk English. They are introduced to the best traditional canons of all fields, to foreign languages, to the disciplined, basic, not politically-adjusted sciences.

---

[2] "Desperately poor" is a no-nonsense phrase used by Barbara Ehrenreich in *Nickel and Dimed: On (Not) Getting By in America*. New York: Henry Holt and Company, a Metropolitan/Owl Book, 2001.

3. Empire-wanters mean to bring up the children of the privileged to the doctrine that we and they will never meet. The young privileged must learn an attractive solemnity about this doctrine. They must learn to make it clear they couldn't be more sorry about poverty, but there it is. A draconian model for indoctrinating privileged youth with total disrespect for the poor is the government of the ancient city-state Sparta. Sparta had been in the 6th century B.C. an open, cultured, and comparatively free-thinking society like Athens. By the 4th century, however, Sparta's privileged class had consciously and deliberately regressed their city-state to the natural, empire formula. Young males were encouraged to hunt and kill members of the they-populace they might find wandering about the surrounding countryside. Young males maintained among themselves a secret police to enforce conformity of thought. Foreigners were no longer allowed to visit Sparta because they might bring with them a liberal exchange of ideas.

4. Empire-wanters want to vitiate all possible checks on the Executive branch. They want to get some conventions in place for punishing dissidents with as little legal obstruction as possible. A side-means for doing this is to slide as much budget as you can over to the military. Anyone wanting to change a democracy to an empire is happy to move all sorts of strange moneys into military pockets. The military, of all the structures in a nation, give an emperor the least grief. By definition soldiers and their officers belong to psychological stage 4–utter loyalty to the top leader or leaders. (See the Stage Development Scheme in the Appendix.)

5. Empire-wanters want to expand the country's control over space outside its present borders—this for two reasons, the first of which is ostensibly practical: one wants to grab more territory for raw or industrialized resources and as a people-and-acreage buffer against other empires present or potential. Second: an addiction to assaulting and invading one's neighbors is a psychological dynamic that one sees in mammals including human beings. It shows up remarkably in third-and fourth-grade boys in school yards. Asian, African, and European history is full of

addicted dictators of our time and the past.

We may resist saying or hearing that bullying others is great fun. The fact is, however, that control for its own sake is an addiction, something the way over-eating is an addiction: it begins as a practicality. One must control some territory or one can't stand up or sit or lie down anywhere in the world. One must eat something or one's organism fails. Eating and controlling territory do not start as addictions.

6. At last, for what is wonderfully called in American slang "power freaks," an empire-wanter typically wants to hold the upper hand even at home. If the family is going to have any incidental, everyday life he wants to dominate it. A small-scale example: one is the head, let us say, of a family of some fundamentalist persuasion. An exercise: let's pretend you are this father. You have just sat down to table with spouse and children. (The memoirs of battered children in fundamentalist cultures regularly reveal the fact that the father times much of his bullying for family mealtimes.) As you drop hands after the prayer which you, as head of the family, have just led, you glance around at those edgy, vapid faces. They are all scared. The beast in you rouses up. What colorless wimps they all look! You do not put words to this, since the onset of the urge is largely unconscious in people who allow themselves regularly to bully, and all the more unconscious in people who believe that they dominate others for the sake of a savior.

I never realized the intense enjoyment of bullying until I watched a Lutheran Church Worship and Growth Committee contrive to drive their pastor out of a church. None of us could compass the pure malignity of the three men making the move. We knew that they had asked the Bishop to help them get rid of the pastor but the Bishop had refused. Well, they were men, not mice. They wanted to get rid of that pastor because he preached that Christian churches should welcome to their memberships every human being who wanted to come in. A couple of desperately poor people had entered our church. You could see them there in the sanctuary, with the clothes, the hair, the gum chewing and all. The Worship and Growth Committee persevered and chased the pastor out. What is curious about it is how passionate the Committee were. They used the language of people about to climb Mount Everest. Those men were in love with dominating others. Dominating others is rather like social climbing. Their feeling wasn't just an unfortunate penchant: it was an example of a passion that breaks out in unexpected places and from the minds of unexpected people. A dominator will classically describe his or her passion as a mission, with the thrust of religious language.

7. An empire-wanter constantly urges and shoves to get freedom for the business community from restraints of environmental legislation, freedom from the expense of caring for employees' livelihood, freedom from the expense of safety legislation for those using or near heavy equipment, and reducing as much as possible whatever health provision a company is required to provide.

And what, likely, are the heart's longings of republic-preservers? The only good use of making such a list is for us to read this as if each of us were a shadow cabinet. What is my true goal if so?

1. I want my country to cooperate with other nations instead of dominating them.

2. I want to plan to share out many more riches with the they, the bottom-paid and already psychologically enfeebled they. I want to remove many of the tax loopholes of the rich and use those moneys to buy small-class education for the country's public schools. If each kid sat K through 12 in classes of 8 or fewer they could be educated just as well as kids in private county day schools and boarding schools are now educated. They, if given 12 years of we-type group process—small groups led by sympathetic teachers—would come to speak and think amazingly like we members. Other sharing: I want all persons with diagnoses of cancer to get equal and free treatment for it. The same goes for other medical situations, including mental illness.

3. Basically: I want the America of Katherine Lee Bates's "America" (O Beautiful for Spacious Skies) especially in this verse:

O beautiful for pilgrim feet
Whose firm impassioned stress
A thoroughfare for freedom beat
Across the wilderness.
America, America!
God mend thine every flaw;
Confirm thy soul in self-control,
Thy liberty in law.

This would be an America that practices constraints in every sphere. For example, the Congress would be constrained honorably to pay up our dues to the UN.

4. I would like to change our psychological expectations of one another. I would like to ask Americans to make sacrifices for certain ideals that they secretly hold but are too afraid of their workplace colleagues to express. Two hundred years ago Alexis de Tocqueville was amazed at how afraid American males are of one another.

5. I would like the most modern philosophies, in addition to the age-old wisdom, taught to all American young people. "Modern," here, means group psychology brilliantly developed in the 1980s, the neurology of the 1990s and 2000s instead of the outdated, never-substantiated psychological determinism of the 1940s. Every kid should learn at least one foreign language because it makes ideation flexible and builds a respect for people who are different. In this country educators forever gas on about "diversity." Learning a foreign language teaches it experientially. People who speak a foreign language at ages 4-7 do not jeer at foreign ideas just because they are foreign.

6. I would like my government to do what foreign governments have done when the housing lack for the poor worsens: corner some public moneys for cheap housing and get it built.

Feeding the Army in Iraq cost over $600,000 a day in 2002, likely more now. The army should come home and our civilian poor should be housed.

Such a list is straight shadow cabinet. That whole notion of imagining oneself as shadow cabinet is curiously enlivening. It highlights and clicks on one's own least cynical ideas. We have so much cynicism slapping around like jetsam in our minds. We rightly don't pay it much attention, the way a swimmer doesn't pay much attention when stroking his or her way through used plastic bags, floating tongue depressors, wads of waxed paper smeared with catsup in Long Island Sound. The swimmer keeps on with his or her crawl or breast-stroke, valiantly not stopped by the junk, but the smell of junk and touch of junk is disheartening. If we make a list of our own public goals for our country it cheers us up despite all the bad behavior around the place. Maybe it cheers us up *because* of all the bad behavior around the place.

A second reason is that the goals on your list may be the goals of actual candidates for office. No matter how candidates may glitz up their speeches with sparkles, the goals you listed may be theirs.

We live in a lying culture just now. The United States need not always be a culture where top business people regularly and frequently are caught bilking others and then lying their way out of blame, but that is what our culture is like now. It is wise for us to know that. We need to maintain a lot of bad news in our heads so we won't be fools, but we should also maintain our own best convictions.

Whatever is said to the contrary, the wanting to be an emperor and to trip up and knock down a free and law-abiding country into an empire is a passion. Some people have that passion. Alcibiades, Alexander, Ceausescu, Stalin, Hitler. It is one of those human passions that at the beginning glides so delicately one doesn't always notice the grass stems moving above it, but it is there.

First the paranoiacs shriek and point to it—but then, paranoiacs are always shrieking and pointing at something, so we ignore them.

Then the rest of us begin to notice.

CHAPTER 4

8 normal psychological dynamics the very mention of which infuriates a lot of people: escapes from painful realizations

Refusing to listen to low-level, background anxiety (Black noise)
Defending oneself against new painful abstract concepts even if willing to accept new painful perceptions
Pitying ourselves when the suffering of others spoils our own peaceful backwater
Hiding in easy patriotism from internationalism
Hiding from philosophical life by enjoying our hobbies
Hiding in a nostalgic view of the past, by dint of which one need pay no attention to the psychological or ethical ideas illustrated in that past
Hiding from both religious and political activism by insisting that all great acts belong in the past
Self-congratulation over one's own lifestyle, a kind of defendedness against political anxiety that is common to all classes of people

Refusing to listen to low-level, background anxiety (Black noise)
        Women both lecture and write warm fuzzy remarks about breastfeeding babies. Because breast feeding or not breast feeding is a nearly-medical issue, involving nutritional and psychological attachment issues and so forth, much of the writing about it is advocacy. The essays and whole books about it usually want to sell the idea, so to speak. They focus on the holy feelings between mother and child. The early kind of feminism even made much of the "relationality" of mother and child. All such ideas are valuable They have done noble work in halting the peculiar sort of 1920s and 1930s social climbing which dictated that it was less peasant-like to bottle feed formula than nurse your own babies.
        Like most good advice, we've heard it before. The advisors are right. When all the focus is on the simple, broad outlines of a

topic like breast feeding, however, we forget to analyze why we do some of what we do. As I look back on that nursing-mother period of my life, I realize that I did not ask myself—not even once—why it might be that escape reading was the reading of choice for breast feeding.

I knew the conventional wisdom. Young mothers put up with so much sleep deprivation that they feel heroic. They deeply know they have a right not to strain their brains when breast feeding. Right enough. Still, it seems thick-headed of me and my friends not to have been asking ourselves and one another, "If we are doing 'escape reading' while nursing our babies, what are we escaping *from?*" If we had asked one another that question I expect we'd have grinned and said "Escape from having to pay attention to nervous-making drivel, what do you think?" We would have thought, for the love of heaven why analyze anything that everyone already under-stands? Analysis of why one did anything was anathema to liberal-arts graduates anyway. At my college psychology and sociology were regarded as gut, not thinking courses.

Too bad, since the usual liberal-arts approach to neo-conservatism—that is, wringing of hands and the howl, "How could they etc." and "I just can't understand how they could do etc...."—is a useless way to respond to any ethics dilemma. We will be stuck right there if we refuse to think psychologically. Thinking psychologically means making some guesses about why anyone does a certain thing and then trying the guesses for fit. Psychological thinking is never much good unless one looks closely at the particulars of the case. For example, if we all have agreed to do only escape reading while nursing babies we will never figure out why we decided such a thing unless we identify exactly what kinds of books count as good escape reading? We can leave out the obvious physical considerations such as that the book has to be light enough to hold in one hand and to lay on the baby's stomach long enough to turn the page and then raise the book to read again.

As soon as I made the list below, it was perfectly clear what I was trying to escape from.

1. The story should be set before August, 1945.

2. Stories set in England, France, Germany, Norway, or Russia were best, but American fiction was acceptable provided the writing was elegant. (Mickey Spillane didn't make the cut.)

3. The stories should have absolutely no social protest in them.

4. All privileged or upper-class characters in the stories should have stalwart, endearing characteristics. They should not be either cynics or slobs. The perfect short story of this kind was J.D. Salinger's "For Esme—With Love and Squalor." Both the war-disturbed soldier and the little English girl were sentient people. Neither was rapacious.

5. If the novel was British, the royal family shouldn't show up deplorable in any way. If the novel was a war novel, all captains and crews of RAF Bomber Command or similar organizations should be reasonably patriotic and absolutely honorable about their work.[1] Principal protagonists were still gentlemen, not liars, and privileged people had enough character to practice some noblesse oblige. Women fell in love with men but didn't tweak their own sexual prowess to make fast moves. No army or air force or navy characters wasted young men's lives for the sake of their own ego trips. Norman Mailer's *The Naked and the Dead* didn't make the cut because General Cummings in it devised inexcusably ill-judged assaults on Japanese positions just because he wanted personal acclaim. Because I believed the psychologically stupid style of comment on that book—that it was such a wonderful window into the Pacific War from the fighting man's point of view—I accidentally read it before realizing it was literature with an ethical message. It's horrible to think of how much literature probably passes under people's eyes the way pearls get taken for corn by swine. I kept absolutely clear of Dwight Macdonald's courageous essays in *The New Yorker* and elsewhere about the daytime flights of the U.S. Eighth Army Air Force against far-flung oil fields and industrial

---

[1] Len Deighton, a popular World War II author, gave his heroes good character and his commissioned villains satisfyingly rotten character. *Bomber*, a book published long enough after World War II to be against war generally, is the perfect case. The author did not cynically make his leading character a trickster.

targets. I knew but hastily dropped all work by John Le Carré because its characters were victims of Cold War moles and the like. The Cold War made very poor escape reading.

6. All fiction had to be serious fiction—not snappy, tongue-in-cheek social comment of a sort from supercilious authors. That is, I wanted to escape into a story in the old classic way.

7. Some of my chosen escape reading was re-reading. I reread *Anna Karenina*, two of Jane Austen's novels, *Mrs. Dalloway* of Virginia Woolf's. I carefully avoided *A Room of One's Own* and *Three Guineas* because they were change-agent reading, certainly very opposite to escape reading.

I generally avoided the then recent American writing because by the time I was raising children Americans had been watching TV instead of reading for a decade and a half. Thousands of words had already dropped out of the working vocabulary of American writers.[2]

This aesthetic loss of beautiful writing served to blind me to a more important reason for preferring older work to recent work. That is, I assumed I was merely disappointed with the dull language of much recent American writing. I recognized that disappointment and my own snobbery to go with it but I didn't look any further. Only decades after all that escape-reading-while-breastfeeding-babies did I wake up to certain underlying psychological reasons for my list.

---

[2] A common way we lose words in present-day America is in eliding two words into one word, thus losing some fine-tuned word in the dropped word. Nowadays a hyphen is a dash as well as a dash being a dash. "Cynical" now stands for "pessimistic" as well as for cynical. Actually, most Americans don't know the word pessimistic any more. They also don't know that "cynical" once meant "doesn't give a damn whether virtue or sleeze conquers" whereas pessimistic meant "doesn't hold much hope for virtue being able to hold the line against sleeze." Those two very different concepts are now slapped together under one word. The word "concerned" now means worried or outraged or mildly annoyed or empathically saddened. This means that language is considerably more approximate than before. A parallel in arithmetic would be rolling together the numbers 4 and 5 so that when one added 2 and 3 the sum would be allowed to stand as "4 or 5, you know what I mean." A parallel in social work would be combining "enablers," "co-dependents," and "substance abusers" into a single word. Until about 1970 Latin words used in English still had singular and plural forms—one phenomenon, two phenomena; one bacterium, two bacteria; one alumnus or alumna, two alumni or alumnae. Those distinctions now seem quaint, but readers who like some exactitude relish books whose authors make distinctions for the sake of clarity.

The Minnesota Historical Society Press, a publishing house approximately 35 times the size of the next largest state historical society press, asked me to review several memoirs in the series they had planned. I read memoirs of Minnesota pioneering life, recent Minnesota farming life, Native American life in Indian schools and on the reservations, the lives of civil-minded idealistic Minnesota women and how they were openly insulted by Minnesota legislators. Next I put my hands on what reviews had been written about these memoirs. I now noticed something that irritates moralists whenever they meet it: none, not one, of the reviews mentioned the gross injustices reported or good-temperedly narrated in the memoirs. Reviewers, apparently, were one hundred percent indifferent to the ethical revelations in these memoirs. The reviewers saw them only as marvelous windows into the past and the just-past present.

I decided to telephone and write each of the authors if I could reach them to ask if there were other reviews that I somehow hadn't got my hands on. And please would they tell me, had they seen any reviews that remarked on the ethical issues touched on in their books? Well, no, now I brought it up, they didn't guess they had. The tone of two of the authors told me perhaps I was being difficult. "But why would the reviewers fuss over ethical issues?" the authors seemed to say. "I myself didn't focus on what you seem to be talking about."

I felt reminded of Chekhov's comment about people good-naturedly taking their dead to be buried and making no complaints. (See the passage from "Gooseberries" in chapter 2.)

If I had had a better background in classic Greek literature I shouldn't have been indignant or even surprised. The classical Greek playwrights gave us all a wonderful century of classic literature—which first and foremost, by definition, had to do with humankind's raw feelings versus humankind's prescience about better principles that we could be living by if (a) we had better character or (b) we were taught to long for it. That was the message of those of the greatest writers. Then, with Menander and other comedians of a new kind, Greek taste changed. Even the so-impressive Athenians now wanted sit coms. They wanted to think only about private lives. They were no longer fascinated with thinking up ways to improve on their city state. They now liked vivid sensation for its own sake.

I looked over the Minnesota memoirists' books again. This time I made a list of anecdotes in them that made me feel either angry or anxious. It was a long mixed list: over half was what you'd expect—loss of beautiful farmland to industry or to wildly expanding acreages in Midwestern farming between 1900 and 1980; loss of cultural heritage as pioneer families' exhaustion took its toll—the violins remained leant against the cabin corners, the family singing withered or dropped off, the reading of Old Country (principally Scandinavian) poets and novelists fell away.

Another half of what made me very uneasy was the background presence of general doom. The memoirists seemed to be manfully putting up with general doom. Curiously, every single one of those memoirists was a good sport about any feelings of doom. They had those feelings, but they civilly didn't blame anyone for them.

Here are five of the causes of feelings of doom.

1. Shame that the United States dropped a second A-bomb on the Japanese people.

2. Resentment not just of the world's overpopulation but of American overpopulation.

3. Loss of both natural beauty and architectural beauty in our countryside.

4. Resentment at the rise of upper-class criminality, against which in the 1980s and 1990s so little serious protest was put forth.

5. Hatred of the furtherance of capitalism past its point of diminishing life-enhancement returns. (That is, in early stages, capitalism did well by citizens' lifestyle—well, at least by the lifestyle of white citizens and other comparatively privileged people in the United States. Now, however, in its latter stages, capitalism has meant more birth defects, less accessible health insurance, architecture designed to crumble once the first mortgage has expired, and other bad work of the kind that ordinary people without economics backgrounds easily notice.)

I realized I was looking at the specific anxieties that had years before dictated my idea of what made good escape reading. For the first time I actually identified what an educated reader wants to escape from.

Right away, however, it became clear that my five causes of wrath or anxiety or moral outrage, whichever got my attention at a particular moment, were the same five causes that millions of Americans have protested about since 1945. I revised my planned review of the Minnesota memoirists. It was requested by the American Journal of Higher Education. My essay explained how beautifully the memoirs illustrated five widespread anxieties of Americans. [The editors of the American Journal of Higher Education rejected the review. See Appendix for the full essay.]

We decided to call these five, plus any similar anxieties that people try to keep out of mind, *black noise.* "White noise" is planned buzzing in thin-walled apartment buildings without which one would hear too much from people in adjoining apartments. After a few minutes' exposure to white noise one doesn't hear it any more because the brain refuses to report sense impressions that stay the same. The stunning classic case of this refusal is the so-called "snow blindness" experienced by people who have spent too long traversing arctic plains whose horizon never varies and whose skies and snow cover are equally white. The eyes have actually not gone blind. The brain, following a common pattern of sense-to-meaning relaying, refused to send in the same dumb report—more white. Everything white.

If black noise is to moral dismay what white noise is to sensory dismay, then a steady buzz, inside ourselves, of fear or resentment that never weakens or strengthens, and upon which we make no decisions and take no actions, might well make the cortex re-entrant system (discussed in Chapter 5) stop sending reports back and forth along the pathways of our core consciousness. If the authors as well as the reader-reviewers of the memoirs are more or less neutral to ethical outrages reported in the text, perhaps the cortex, getting no response to those ethical outrages writes off the feeling of outrage.

Another likelihood depends on a side-theory of the neurology of re-entry activity in the cortex. The brain's pathways of feelings that we are conscious of don't always consist of the same gangs of neurons. When a neurologist uses the phrase "core consciousness' he may be referring to several quickly waked and activated neighborhoods of neurons which have just got word of some news from outside coming in by way of the sense. The neurons selected to respond vary from one individual news report to another. Some neurons get dropped off. Others, from other parts of the brain, get waked up to fire. The brain doesn't stay conscious of everything it gets word of just because it was once conscious of it. If the brain once surmised that overpopulation might well be an aggravator of crime, a cause of crowding, a cause of spoilt landscape, a factor in poor pay being given for labor done, a cause of languishing affection between villagers whose villages are now suburbs quarreling over the clean water outlook, the cortex would eventually drop consciousness of the idea if the organism (that's us—the organism) wouldn't or couldn't do anything about it. The brain would relegate it to unconsciousness.

We should distinguish between "relegate to unconsciousness" and "go into denial." I personally have relegated to unconsciousness the issue of whether or not to keep to the right on United States roadways. A useful behavior (keeping to the right) can be done without having to reevaluate it. Nuclei below our cortex reliably handle thousands and thousands of daily decisions of the kind without bothering our consciousness about it. Thank goodness. It does not mean we have gone into denial about keeping to the right.

The human mind appears to slide black noise—overpopulation, shame of one or another cruelty committed by the United States, and so forth—off the pathways of consciousness for the while—the way an army with somewhere to go is likely to push a truck with a broken axle off into the ditch.

Black noise is the phrase we will use in this book to mean an assortment of back-burner anxieties or hatreds or other unpleasantnesses. Sometimes one needs to not get distracted from black noise lest one spend a lifetime flitting from one "concern" to another. There are people whose whole day seems to be made up of whining over various black noise items. Some of them cheer up when they drink alcohol. They stop grousing. They shake off their constant consciousness of background anxieties. They seem to follow other people's line of thought better. Goodness, perhaps they should drink more, people say with ironic faces. Others do the opposite. All day long they accomplish all sorts of useful committee tasks in their workplace or on behalf of society. In the evening, if you give them a strong cup of sweet tea or a nice bump of alcohol, they suddenly appear to remember and express a long series of back-burner angers you never knew they felt. For them, generally low-range black noise suddenly gets into strong focus when they take any kind of exterior stimulus. Their minds are like deer struck motionless by auto headlights. They are cognitively stuck for the time. I don't think these random victims of black noise are in panic.

A minute ago, let us say, a middle-range conservative investment counselor stood in front of the bookshelves affably greeting his aunt who is spending the night in town. The hostess has gone for drinks. The host is making the aunt and this particular guest feel welcome. Lydia returns with a tray of drinks. People pick up the glasses. Someone gets toasted.

The broker suddenly says, "OK if I bring up something kind of serious?"

"Take it away, Bill," the host says.

The guest looks around in a demanding way, not wild-eyed, no eyes rolling or any of that reality-TV rot. Still, the glance is demanding. The guest is gathering your attention by force of eyeball.

"Well, here's the damnedest thing," he says. "I dreamed last night about Nagasaki. Well, hell, anyone can have a dream about Nagasaki, but here's what's getting to me. Why did they bomb Nagasaki? After the A-bombing of Hiroshima, the Japanese made several pleas for peace. OK—OK, I'm getting there—here is what is bothering me: did someone want to drop that second bomb so badly they couldn't keep themselves from giving the order? Was there so much money tied up in the manufacture of those two bombs that someone couldn't stand to waste half of it by not dropping the second one on Japanese people?

"I woke cold and terrified. But I had lots to do today, speaking of which, please don't let me forget to tell you about your Rittenhouse stuff, Lydia,..so I just did my usual stuff all day. But now—well, looking around at all of you and thinking I would get you to tell me about this wild vacation idea you guys have put together—suddenly... Well, suddenly, I started telling you about Nagasaki."

"Yes and why shouldn't you?" The host says. "That damned business."

"I'm glad you did," Lydia says. "Thank you, Bill."

The visiting aunt smiles encouragingly but doesn't say anything just now. She is old and the martini they mixed for her has hit her visual and motor cortices and is cantering along the pathway of her thoughts, sticking a little here and there, the way even the most spirited horse finds a viscous trail affects its gait. She has a philosophical nature, which old people should have, so of course she plans to say something commendatory to Bill, her kind, red-faced nephew of fifty, but not just this minute. She is savoring the martini hit for just now. She used to jog so she has the common sense not to waste any dopamine effect her brain is willing to put up.

In the field of literature we have some geniuses, short story writers mainly, who are good at showing how human beings "accommodate" ongoing anxieties (to use John Kenneth Galbraith's word "accommodate" meaning bite the bullet whether they should or should not bite it.) Many of Chekhov's improvident characters trot along rather like pleasant dogs at their ordinary lives. They are owned by someone other than themselves, or they believe they are being controlled by someone or something other than themselves. Or perhaps they are just psychologically *halt*, so to speak, as in "the halt and the blind." Like sensible prisoners, they think in fragments. If you really have no control over things deeper than your week of duty if you have work or your weekend hobbies you are wise to think in pleasant fragments—to enjoy the smell of fresh wood shavings from your saber saw. Prisoners, to live any sort of decent life, need to make sure they adapt to the prison schedule all right, but they have to be equally careful to daydream in ways that can heighten the aesthetics of their minds yet keep all justice issues in the smallest fragments. People living in high rises sometimes manage it: they are ready with aesthetic observations, small ones about small things, the smell of autumn coming again, so when their family come to visit they find the old man or woman hale and enjoying old age.

No one in literature so far as I know, absolutely no one, understands the piquancy of utterly hopeless ordinary low-key conscious feelings better than Chekhov. Chekhov hasn't got Tolstoy's hankering for holiness. This makes Chekhov sometimes more accurate. Chekhov doesn't seem to have to convince himself that anyone is really 100% wholesome. Peasants aren't wholesome, charming women aren't completely wholesome. If you run through a number of Chekhov's stories you find a quiet pointless day described, and then an explosion of feeling not on a major new issue, but on some misery previously made nothing of. The feeling streams upward about something that has stayed under the radar all day or all week or for years, like Bill's feeling about Nagasaki.[3]

Sometimes black noise should stay just black noise. Sometimes, and this is the distinguishing task of social workers, to help someone see that what appears as black noise—just some back-burner dismay of some sort—should never have been rolled under into unconsciousness as it was. It was a genuine and passionate feeling, but apparently one so out of style or socially ridiculous that the person who had it instinctively decided not to recognize it at the time.

---

[3] The present-day neurologist, Antonio Damasio, q.v., has published a book relating the passionate feelings to ethical concepts pulled together by a brain. It is called *Looking for Spinoza*. See the small bibliography. Damasio has a great interest in how the brain succeeds or fails in collecting the perceptions that come to it—from the outside, from the body, and from its own linkage of remembered values—and then making a general meaning of them. I believe the reason that W. Somerset Maugham was so testy and insulting about Chekhov is that unlike Chekhov (or Damasio), Maugham wasn't philosophically interested in meaning: he was interested in character and in madcap circumstances, but he regarded the question of *meaning* in life, as such, as self-sorry humbug. He once remarked that if people get obsessed with the folly of human nature all the time they will spend their lives "in a constant state of ire." It sounds witty and sensible until one thinks of people savaging a democracy in order to make a fat self-serving empire out of it—is that folly that we should have a sense of humor about or is it something we should feel ire about?

In this chapter we are discussing eight ways that people defend themselves from being conscious of strong feelings about government. Further: the major reason a decent republic has to have government is quite different from the major reason an empire has to have a government.[4]

Remanding our anxiety over certain cruelties or injustices to mere black noise is one such psychological defense. It may be a reason that so much present-day American literature never mentions public cruelties at all. Perhaps the authors have remanded their own feelings about such things to mere black noise. Perhaps their reviewers have done the same.

Defending oneself against new painful abstract concepts even if willing to accept new painful perceptions.
The usual dynamic called "denial" is denial of facts. A less recognized dynamic is that someone agrees to the facts of the case but denies the concept those data point to. An alcoholic agreeably admits to having overdone it last night and the night before and the night before that, but those three pieces of data cause no pain: the abstract idea that he or she is an alcoholic is what would be painful.

Denial of abstract theory seems to run two courses, both a little different from denial of fact. First, some people hate all theory if it is contemporary theory. One can ride in a car on a business trip of some sort and listen to someone in the car point out how spoilt the New England countryside now is with its sprawl of malls and service stations and ugly personal storage sheds and tourist buses up around the "Fall Colors" and so forth. Someone else in the car says. Oh this is nothing. You ought to see Texas. Someone else says something else, something sociable and anecdotal that gives a mental image but proves no particular point. Then, let's say, a tactless sociologist in the car says to the original speaker, "So what are you saying, actually—are

[4] An empire, which wants to expand its borders, has government principally so it can command the armed services to make the expansion happen for the leader or few leaders at the top. A decent republic theoretically is not starting pre-emptive wars, so its main reason for government is for a) the control of criminal domination of some citizens by other citizens and b) designing, financing, and implementing infrastructure.

you saying you find yourself grieving about the overpopulation in New England?"

The speaker, a little mysteriously, feels infuriated, not because the question is probing or rude but because it purports to be drawing an abstract meaning of some sort from what the speaker regarded as a passing remark. The average person, especially if he or she has not learned in college to draw conclusions from small gatherings of data, believes in passing remarks. Social workers and other helping professionals, on the contrary, take scarcely anything for merely "passing remarks." Educated people may allow themselves to feel scornful of people who resist all conceptual thinking, but their scorn is child's play compared to the scorn that an uneducated person can feel for abstract thinkers. Statements of invisible value—abstractions—irritate the "concrete thinker."

When I first went to live in the countryside I kept hearing a remark made that I couldn't exactly fathom. It was "He's too smart for his own good." Whenever I could I asked what that meant, but of course was told "He just is, that's all." The statement wasn't thinking: it was feeling something and the person who felt it, speaking in that scornful voice, wouldn't ever be conscious enough to say, "I feel scorn for abstract thinkers like him and I shan't be sorry if he will come to a bad end."

Nietzsche believed that uneducated classes dislike educated classes and always must: they are cursed, he thought, with a never ending *ressentiment.* I don't think people's hatred of abstract theory always comes of ressentiment. It might come simply of having had too little experience in abstract thinking to have built a taste for it. So far as abstract thinking goes, perhaps one needs more than the few years of high school exposure in order to enjoy it. I have met people who despise anyone who uses metaphor or analogy: it is as if they can spot metaphor and analogy as trail marks of concept thinking. Even if such a concrete-thinking person finally fetched up a generalization to send back to you, since you nagged for one, and even if you praised him or her for doing so, they wouldn't feel gratified. They would feel the way you would feel if praised for eating politely the white meat served you when all your life you have preferred dark and you ate white only out of consideration.

What they feel, I think, is not Nietzsche's ressentiment but social annoyance or perhaps a touch of deprivation. I feel both annoyed and deprived when a scientist begins to write formulae on a blackboard. First I feel stupid, then stricken, and then cross. The moving hand with the chalk reminds me that our species, not dogs or horses or even the brighter members—cats and pigs—writes formulae on blackboards that make other people's faces shine and their voices exclaim, "O yes, damn it all, of course! Why didn't I see that!" That's one expectation of our species that I have been locked out from.

A second reason for defending against concepts, and a much more important one so far as moral growth goes, is the human fear that a new concept coming around might jar loose some old concept we have built our personal philosophy on in the past. It is this dynamic that makes politics a feral subject: somebody is going to use an abstract concept to upset major tenets of my life. Once such a fear takes hold, a person even prefers clearly dishonest schmooze to the sharp blade of this new truth. This happens to groups.

Whole societies prefer agreeable schmooze to any edgy new truth. This generally comes up in matters of religious doctrine and in politics. But occasionally it leaves its mark in science, particularly science as learned by uncourageous people. An English astronomer named James Challis (in Cambridge) was doing a stint of night scanning during the winter of 1845-46. One night he saw the comet called Biela get oddly pear-shaped and at last divide itself into two distinctly separate comets. Challis saw it. Challis apparently went into denial about it. The contemporary wisdom, despite an earlier statement to the contrary by Kepler, was that comets don't split. Meteors yes, comets no.

"...One of the astronomers [Challis] who observed [the now 2 comets that had been one, named Biela], averted his gaze. A week later Challis looked again and found Biela still double. For several more days the cautious Challis hesitated before he announced it to his astronomical colleague. In the mean time, however,

American astronomers in Washington, DC and New Haven…had already staked their claim to the discovery. Challis excused his slowness in reporting the event by saying that he was busy looking for the new planet beyond Uranus."[5]

Challis resisted an idea for the reason that it gainsaid authorities whom he had trusted. Stage development philosophers have found it true that authority-followers do tend to distrust their own thinking as such. To explain very briefly Challis's likely predicament: the neurons on the surface of our eyes send back news to various visual centers at the top of the cortex. They tell the cortex centers that they have seen something novel—for example, a comet splitting in earth's atmosphere. The visual cortex sends this newsbreak widely around the cortex, in great "bands," so to speak, of firing neurons, reciprocally sending the information and receiving responses from other neighborhoods of neurons, and some responses from the nuclei below the cortex. All of this "re-entrant" process takes place in milliseconds from the visual cortex's first having picked up the news.[6] The neurons map for one another what they understand. Those maps, what's more, map to other maps. The neurons receiving the images confer with neurons who have handled past, remembered images on the same or relevant subject. They confer with one another, comparing *qualia*—a philosophy and neurology phrase for the felt values that the brain makes of raw news combined with categorized concepts it has previously made. The neurons are revising the old values or old truths. But let's say at least one of the old truths wasn't truthful. Comets do break up, it turns out. A lively brain that hasn't been inhibited by fear of change will accept the new perception sent in by the eyes, and also accept the meaning that the brain's own millions of neuronal connections have brought to fiery life. Such a spirited, non-damaged brain is lucky: it can go about its magnificent

---

[5] Nigel Calder, *The Comet is Coming!*, New York: The Viking Press, 1980, pages 66-67
[6] For scholarship and much more enchanting descriptions of re-entrant activity of the human cortex please see Antonio Damasio and Gerald M. Edelman references in the bibliography.

work of deriving a better theory to replace the old one since the old one was wrong.

There is a lot of feeling involved in that process! For one thing, our cortex-generated conscious feelings show a genuine penchant for rectitude compared with the mere raw emotions that the body sends up through the amygdala or by other routes. That is, the body's abiding mission is to keep the organism—that's us—steady within the perimeter of our skin and the parameters of our needs for safety and freedom from too much stress, etc. The body sends up its responses to anything new. Here's the sort of conversation the amygdala would make if it made conversation: "What! Something new? Bad! Threatening! Run! No, kill it. If you're not up for killing it the least you can do is pretend you don't see it! If it's there you'd see it. If you don't see it it isn't there!" This last was Challis's choice. He waited some nights before looking at Biela a second time: he didn't want that new information still to be there.

A luckier (for which read "better") cortex, however, receives the body's news but continues to race about its creasy six-layer hood of thinking above the nuclei. It is putting together something infinitely more elegant than the raw emotional responses. Neurons in the cortex, forming a kind of core consciousness, are flying through and through, by electricity, then chemical jump, then electricity again, then chemical jump again, and so forth, through its thickety chemo-electric pathways to give us—the organism, that's us— the admixture of excitement, some dread, perhaps, but most lovely, a trumpeting of new theory—generally speaking, what we call finding new meaning in life.

Well, what's a "good cortex" then? It is a human brain habituated by culture to pay a lot of attention to its re-entrant impressions. (Please see in chapter 5 and also in the Appendix passages from William Wordworth's "Preface to the Lyrical Ballads, Second Edition," 1800.) Wordsworth says that a poet confers more inside his own imagination than with sharp sensations coming in from the outside. The neuroscientist Gerald M. Edelman says the brain "is much more in touch with itself than with anything else." Wordsworth's is the intuitive voice of 200 years ago. Edelman's is the voice of the 21st century reinforcing our confidence in thinking itself.

If James Challis had trusted his own mental (re-entrant) processes he would have been able to equably replace an old, now disproven concept with a new concept.

Challis's story is useful because if we use a Social Work technique and try to guess at what Challis was specifically afraid of we will be using a tool we can use a dozen times a day in our century. We can guess at the specifics of people's fear of truth, case by case. Like any open-minded hypothesizing, our guesses are likely to be wrong. We are especially likely to be wrong about Challis because he lived in the 1840s. We can't be certain about why his mind so nervously defended against the comet's splitting. Certain or uncertain, however, we can make hypotheses. No one can be certain of 21st-century causes of other people's fears, either, but it is important to make hypotheses. For starters, we can pretend we are James Challis.

A serious consideration: perhaps young people want all the authorities in their lives to be loving and parental. They feel a pang upon finding that an old authority in their life has lied to them. If your ego is poorly developed[7] you can hardly make yourself contradict authority. You would sooner say, if you were Challis, that you guess you saw the comet wrong than say, "What I saw proves that what you've told me, Old Respected Teacher, is not true."

The classical instance is the battered child who refuses to reject Dad's teaching. Dad has told two lies that the child believes because Dad is authority. He told this child that he is beating the child because he loves him. That is Lie no. l. Lie no. 2 is that if the child were not being bad, Dad explains, poor Dad would not have to beat him. If there are other children the plot thickens. The not-yet-battered child has watched the loving dad beat his or her older siblings. At last, the child got old enough to be beaten and duly was beaten. If this went on

---

[7] We strongly uphold Dr. Jane Loevinger's idea that egos aren't "strong" or "weak:" they are developed or undeveloped—a very different thing. Loevinger is a stage developmentalist of a determined cast of mind. In her *Ego Development* she again and again shows how the mind is in flux, growing, halting, being blocked, getting free again, growing, etc. The pedestal of her ethics says: people must not be written off as a certain type.

unopposed for six or seven years, the child's brain might well have taken aboard the whole system of Dad's thinking. The child's mind has made a spurious but convincing Unified Philosophy out of it.

Brains want to make unified philosophies but all they have to work with, other than gene-specified basics in themselves, is whatever life their organism (the child, us, or Challis, whomever we are talking about) offers. This is a large part of how citizens become amazingly devoted to leaders of totalitarian countries.[8] School social workers and child psychologists know from experience the tremendous resistance that battered kids' minds put up when the lesson to learn is: you love your dad, your dad may love you, but he was wrong to batter you.

In this book we are more interested in denial of concept than in denial of fact because so very much less attention has been given it. Defendedness from new ideation is common to us all. The only really summoning way to think about it, in my opinion, is to note the moment when someone gives you a concept that for some reason wakes you up to a spurt of irritability or as in the case of Bill the broker, fear. That irritability or fear is very likely a road sign to you: it tells you that you have just heard an idea more elegant, more painful, and more morally demanding of you than your previous assumptions on the same topic.

The child needs to learn that Dad lies. Bill the broker needs to worry, lest, while he and Lydia and Lydia's husband and the nice visiting aunt talk to each other, they should be keeping an eye out for fear their own government might do something along the lines of dropping a second atomic bomb on Japan.

---

[8] See the work of the psychoanalyst Alice Miller, *For Your Own Good* on why the German people flocked so instinctively to Adolf Hitler. Dr. Miller's remarks relate the general practice of beating children in Germany to their adherence, amazing, clammy, illogical adherence, to a dictator. There are fascinating observations of citizens' accommodating cruel, even genocidal, leadership in Eli Sagan's *The Honey and the Hemlock: Democracy and Paranoia in Ancient Athens and Modern America*. New York: Basic Books, 1991

Pitying ourselves when the suffering of others spoils our own peaceful backwater

When I was 25 the poet Marguerite Young told me that all serious writers are Democrats, never Republicans. She said, "Well at least they should be Democrats."[9]

I found that the most stupid, the most arrogant concept I'd ever heard said aloud. Like other young married people, graduate students or not, I didn't spend enough time in solitude to think through any ethics. I took for right or wrong whatever was generally considered right or generally wrong from the people I knew. I had read John Stuart Mill on solitude, even the wonderful passage below, but I didn't apply it to my own life because only two of the people I knew—all of whom were literary and oddly jovial—adjured themselves to actually apply the great ideas we read to real life. You just read those great ideas, that's all. For example, here's John Stuart Mill on solitude:

> "It is not good for man to be kept perforce at all times in the presence of his species. A world from which solitude is extirpated is a very poor ideal. Solitude, in the sense of being often alone, is essential to any depth of meditation or of character, and solitude in the presence of natural beauty and grandeur, is the cradle of thoughts and aspirations which are not only good for the individual, but which society could ill do without."[10]

If I had taken Mill seriously, I might have shortcut across decades of casual conventionality in my life. What a waste! On the other hand, George Orwell wrote in "Why I Write," some axioms (which we have reproduced in the appendix of this book) based on the stages he went through. First, he wrote fast and published all sorts of conventional stuff. Then he wrote aesthetically, all sorts of fanciful meters and rhyme schemes, the

---

[9] At that time people who wrote or hoped to write American literature didn't use the word "creative" at all, especially not in front of "writers" or "writing." The OK word was "serious" at the time.

[10] John Stuart Mill, *Principles of Political Economy*, 1848

kind of thing you learn at Eton where he was studying. Then he wrote energetic journalism. Better. He came into his own voice best, however, years later, when he published his moral fantasies, *Animal Farm* and *1984*. The people I knew except for Marguerite Young and another civil idealist were perfectly confident as they went about writing "beautifully" —who cared about justice? They were young and they wanted to write beautiful literature.

That was then, as they say, and this is now. So why bring it up? Apparently some young literary people are still, despite America's misadventures in immoral foreign policies in the past half-century, so self-oriented that when they hear of torture, starvation, and bombing of civilians, what they feel is pity for *themselves*. Being asked to produce poetry for a book against America's assaults in the Persian Gulf and Afghanistan and Iraq, the editor of the anthology sent in work by people whose work was really pity for themselves. Worse, the poems seemed to be informed by both self-pity and chest-thumping that said, please note how sentient a person I am!

Bruce Bawer, a reviewer noticed, however, that for the most part the poets merely grieved that they themselves had been pulled from private lives without political anxiety into the grievous public awareness that Americans are experiencing.

"A staggering number of poems here follow a single trite formula, presenting the news of war as an unpleasant intrusion upon an (American) life lived in harmony with nature and characterized by a taken-for-granted feeling of safety and tranquility....September 11 changed the world. But it seems not to have penetrated very deeply into the imaginations of many contemporary American poets, who, as this anthology amply demonstrates, continue to go through familiar motions, writing smug, trivial verses in which their principal goal is to proclaim their own sensitivity. This was never enough in the first place, and it is certainly not enough now."[11]

---

[11] Bruce Bawer, "A Plague of Poets," *The Hudson Review*, Volume LVI, 2004.

Perhaps there is no way to speed people through the self-pity-ing stage of being waked up to civic responsibility. Even George Orwell had to work his way through the previous stages—person-al ambition, morals-neutral aestheticism. Writers, as Wordsworth said, confer more with themselves inside their minds than they confer with others around them: perhaps it is all the harder for them to even think up an active life as a citizen. They would have to drop their academic belief that no-politics-is-OK.

I pretend I am one of those young poets whom Bawer, the reviewer, was so disgusted with. If I listened to Bawer and got so far as confessing that until this moment I didn't care much about the Afghanistani dead, I would realize, the way you realize you are going to be doing hard work when you pick up a tool so heavy that it is cold to your hand, that I was being asked to take up for one side or another of all public issues for the rest of my life. I would have to be either for or against whatever United States laws got made or abandoned. I would have to be for or against wars gone to or wars not gone to. I would have to be for or against the removal of infrastructures currently benefiting poor people and children. I would have to totter to my feet, so to speak.

Gardens don't happen of themselves, but jungles do. Virtue doesn't happen of itself. Time doesn't just pass and gradually empires become democratic. A democracy happened because of Solon and Cleisthenes deliberately standing up for the rights of those who were vulnerable. (Please see Chapter 3)

The poets Bruce Bawer scolded at were simply self-serving Americans like millions of us who certainly don't want to spoil our lives by leaving what is leisurely and beautiful in order to feel empathic pain.

Hiding in easy patriotism from internationalism

A point people don't think of often: love of one's country is one of the most pleasant of the mild range of feelings. Serving one's country is of course a very different matter, and generally involves likelihood of getting maimed or killed when you are doing it. Just loving one's country, however, is awfully nice. It has only one serious drawback. That is, that most human beings live outside the bounds of your country, whatever your country. Even if you are an Indian or a Chinese, most human beings live outside your borders. Therefore, if we decide to regard those foreigners as either landscape or as enemies, we have made a category in our minds of people we do not love and don't intend to love.

That is practical enough. Why love these billions of people you will never meet?

The trouble here is that each brain wants to make a Unified Philosophy of life. It wants to do it even if culturally balked or pitifully badly educated. It will do it. We have all heard dangerous, even appalling philosophies expressed by people who one can only hope will never hold office, never even get to be village dog catcher, because they would be so cruel.

The key to this issue of philosophies is the word philosophy itself, which contains the Greek word for love, philos. Stage-development theorists and neuroscientists both give wonderful evidence that the brain wants to love life. It is curious and wants to learn much more than it needs to know for only practical reasons. It wants to think about the whole world. It wants to contemplate the Milky Way. The enchantment of this is that everything it learns about it tends to feel some affection for.

At its best the brain is not only internationalist but supra-terrestrial. The psychological drawback to patriotic feelings, then, is that they tend to make a little fence around what we love. Patriotism as an issue isn't worth the trumpeting about it that fundamentalist and non-educated politicians give it, nor is it worth the disdain that so many peace and justice people give it. It's like the smell of pine at Christmas. It is a nice thing.

Hiding from philosophical life by enjoying our hobbies

Hobbies are the great distractor from fear of old age, fear of death, and in pre-teens and teenagers the fear of the whips and scorns of our peers. They are a wonderful escape. They are by definition a subsidiary activity in our lives. They don't make our daily bread for us. If they did we would call them our jobs. They usually involve no abstract thought. Nothing about doing a neat job, measurements and the mortice cuts, of timber framed house building reminds one of the injuries that nations do other nations. Nothing about gardening, even the kind of year-round behind-the-lines gardening (compost prep and land shaping, propagating, and the like) reminds us of the injuries our nation does any other nation's people. Sightseeing in other lands is the privileged person's equivalent to mall shopping. You would think the travelers would be aware of depredations by the United States when they look over kiosks in Reykjavik and Paris, but which half-a-hundred Americans actually know French well enough to read editorials against our position in Iraq? And which two or three Americans can read Morgenblad well enough to pick up on Icelandic indignation about the United States? Experienced travelers—hobbyists who travel—learn the museum-goer's technique for being defended against unpleasant insights. They travel for interest. Interest does not mean growth in compassion. Interest means a pleasant sense of slightly novel occasion, slightly novel hotel styles, and slightly novel geography. The expectation of travel-hobbyists is that along with galleries, museums, and historical sights, one will enjoy a glance or two at the ordinary people at work. Their work will be picturesque, especially if they are using hand tools or 1950s farm machinery instead of 2000s equipment. One sees best what one expects to see so one comes back with good-tempered recall on what one saw and heard.

Hiding in hobbies is a genuine grace to people who don't feel very successful in school, city, or workplace. We know how the "nerd" of middle-school life gets terribly good at in-line skating or skate-boarding or some offbeat sport or an interest in some odd corner of scholarship. The most marvelous case of nerd-makes-good was a thirteen-year-old girl I met whose family had lived in Pakistan for years and years. We were having a reunion dinner. She was eating in a soldierly way, paying no attention to the grownups' talk. She handled her fork and knife like an Englishwoman taken prisoner—keeping the formalities but not pretending to enjoy what wasn't enjoyable. Since I was the host I eventually asked her across the table what her favorite after-or outside-of- school activity was. She stopped eating and regarded me with unblinking eyes and soldierly attention. She

told me, but others heard and the room grew quiet and atten-
tive, that she had been regularly helping to milk cobras of their
venom. My children were mesmerized. We all were. She went
on about it. She knew how the venom would be prepared for
medical and epidemiological use. She kept talking and we all
kept listening. At last her mother cut in and said, "That's good.
Thank you" in a pointed way. I kind of smiled. I meant to smile,
anyhow. She gave me a last cooperative, soldierly glance, as a
just-dismissed sergeant might. She picked up her fork and knife
and finished her plate. This was a kid who'd picked up hobby
expertise and clearly had saved herself, from whatever she
needed or didn't need saving from.

Stay-at-home mothers, no matter how scrupulous their care
and passionate their love for their young children, learn compli-
cated side-activities. They learn to make bookshelves whose
shelves are routed into the uprights, not just free-set on plastic
tabs. Serious hobbyists line up hours and hours of ethics-neutral
activities in a week.

The most touching case of saving oneself through hobby
was reported about crazy people in small towns by two careful,
intricate sociologists, Arthur J. Vidich and Joseph Bensman.

"Aside from sheer incapacity to deal with the problem (living in a small town where one is mentally or
otherwise deficient) there are certain socially stylized
ways of finding release from the psychological ten-
sions. For some individuals a patter of avoidance
based on a withdrawal from the life of the community
can provide a basis for adjustment. Some individuals
pursue idiosyncratic hobbies or other forms of highly
private activities; others make a fetish of pets; one is
totally engaged in the collection and collation of the
performance records of twenty years of athletic
heroes; another builds innumerable birdhouses which
he stores in a shed. It is characteristic of some members of the old aristocracy to withdraw for years into
the private sanctuary of the home, during which time
they may be seen by only a handful of other people.

As a class, the aristocrats withdraw from the affairs of the community and live in a private world made up of their own vanishing set."[12]

Hiding in hobbies is not damaging to anyone, unless the hobbyist turns his or her whole life into the hobby. People made anxious by the various challenges of societal life sometimes slide into this. At some level they have given up being whole people who can bear any variety of impressions coming in. A hobbyist by definition controls the subjects attended to, and thus can keep variety far away. In Chekhov's story "Gooseberries," quoted from earlier, the author inveighs against people retiring into single-issue thinking or single-interest lifestyles.

"It is a common saying that a man needs only six feet of earth. But six feet is what a corpse needs, not a man. It is also asserted that if our educated class is drawn to the land and seeks to settle on farms, that's a good thing. But these farms amount to the same six feet of earth. To retire from the city, from the struggle, from the hubbub, to go off and hide on one's own farm—that's not life, it is selfishness, sloth, it is a kind of monasticism, but monasticism without works. Man need not six feet of earth, not a farm, but the whole globe, all of Nature, where unhindered he can display all of the capacities and peculiarities of his free spirit."[13]

What Chekhov is talking about here is the ideal case, the needs of a full-minded, culturally and psychologically lucky human being. Not everyone can step up to that plate.

Hiding in a nostalgic view of the past, by dint of which one need pay no attention to the psychological or ethical ideas illustrated by that past

[12] Arthur J. Vadich and Joseph Bensman, *Small Town in Mass Society: Class Power, and Religion in a Rural Community,* Rev. edition, with a Foreword by Michael W. Hughey and an Afterword by Arthur J. Vadich, Urbana: University of Illinois Press, 2000, page 288.
[13] Anton Chekhov, in "Gooseberries."

Literature is read more than history, and scarcely anyone reads literature primarily for what it can tell us of human moral behavior. Most of us who love it love it for the story because the story takes us away, away, into another world.

One can read *Remains of the Day*[14] without even noticing that it is about a man who abdicates from human opinion of Nazism because he is of the British servant class who believed they had no right to develop political opinion at all. Servants were allowed only loyalty to the upper-class householders they worked for. Yet people read the book and even saw the film, rapt at this vivid picture of the past. The film showed the pro-Nazi Englishman childishly practicing his German past participles on the two German servant girls he had hired, looking at them subserviently as some people look at their language teachers. Within a week of that, he discovered they were Jewish, and over other people's protests, sent them back to Germany where they would either immediately or in the course of time be murdered and burnt up. The childish expression on the man's face as he spoke to those girls was very great cinema. The movie could be taught at a graduate school of political science as curious evidence in people's refusal to think politically.

Hiding in nostalgia, however, is an addictive psychodynamic. If we get the habit of reading about the past or seeing film about the past and allowing ourselves to feel only nostalgia, the mind lets nostalgia agglomerate other latent feelings to itself.

Hiding from both religious and political activism by insisting that all great acts belong in the past

The past is seen as simply back when, when things were chaotic. Things are stable now—we no longer *live by* those old heroisms—we just *celebrate* some of them.

An old, imaginative, inventive, scholarly academic American had just died. Gisela Konopka had built and run the Institute for Adolescent Girls at the University of Minnesota. We went to the gigantic memorial service for her. It was a kind of celebration which American academics are used to. Many speakers sat wait-

---

[14] Ishiguro, Kazuo, 1988, New York: Vintage Books, (A division of Random House, Inc.)

ing their turn on the raised dais. People from various fields were invited to speak, not only to honor Gisa Konopka, but to represent the spread of people her life had, as they said a dozen times during that service, "touched on."

We therefore were convened in a lecture hall of the modern, vigorous, half-athletic, half-secular/spiritual type. It had huge window space giving natural light. We were sitting in an intellectualized version of a gym—vast, democratic in a slant, brainsy kind of way—a pleasant large space. The speakers sat or stood in one corner at the front, instead of dead center. Beautiful chased steel beams showed overhead. There were musical instruments. The strings players sat where we could not only hear but see them.

Everyone had something to say about Gisa. Everyone said they admired her humane ideas. Everyone said they admired her spirited way of relating to people. Good thing. She did have humane ideas and she did relate to people in a spirited way.

This is the 21st century, however, and personal courage is out of style. A half-century earlier at least four or five of all those speakers would have mentioned the fact that Gisela Konopka and a few of her friends in Germany, when they were very young, had hidden Jews and got numbers of them safely out of Germany. Gisa herself had been questioned by the Gestapo.

Questioned by the Gestapo! How many people in that huge gym full for Gisa's memorial service, expect to experience anything so terrifying as being questioned by the Gestapo?

For whatever reason not one speaker mentioned that she had been interrogated by the Gestapo and had not given names away. Courage must be very out of style. People kept repeating how Gisa made you feel worthy when she talked to you. Public relations or sociable kindness is still in style, apparently.

The two of us walked out finally, too uneasy to break bread with everyone. If Gisa's courage didn't even interest any of her eulogists, and perhaps she is one of only six or seven people in Minneapolis who have experienced such scary stuff as a result of saving lives, does this mean that what she did is not a model for us because bravery is something out of the past, nothing to do with life today? If it is, then fewer people likely are practicing bravery than otherwise would, which means it will be uphill work standing up against a stiffer and stiffer police state if we get one.

The most classical case of this loss of courage because of its being something just from the past, no longer relevant, is Christianity. This religion was once practiced at great cost. It is now not practiced; rather, it is celebrated. The Eucharist is a partial reenactment of the old passions scrupulously carried out as "celebration." Just because you receive the Eucharist no one expects you to stand up alone for Jesus's ideas.

Somewhat lost in schmooze, relationship consciousness, and gentle ways with group discussions, Christianity is small beer these days. Not entirely. The Roman Catholic Church at last canonized an Austrian who refused to serve in the Nazi army, Franz Jägerstätter, a genuine Christian martyr of our time.

The Christian discomfort with its passionate past is an odd psychological phenomenon that may or may not be related to people's not mentioning Gisela Konopka's bravery in the past. In the Charismatic Renewal of 1965 and the years following, many "mainstream" church leaders insulted those who had experienced what was called receiving the "gifts" of the Holy Spirit—namely, speaking in tongues and healing. Conservative churchmen pointed out that that kind of behavior was OK for those being described in the New Testament book of *Acts*, but that was then and this is now.

Perhaps dissociating oneself from the past with all its demanding high-mindedness, trying not to talk under torture, trying to stand alone for justice, that sort of thing, comes naturally. We have our post-day-care social life. Our places of business, our classrooms, don't ask us, are people being cruelly treated somewhere? Getting and staying conscious of cruelty going on at this very moment is probably an acquired taste.

A last kind of defendedness against political anxiety that is common to all classes of people: self-congratulation over one's own lifestyle

Setting store by one's own lifestyle is probably a cultural

product of people's watching so many TV ads as they see. Anything one does hours and hours of a day tends to become a practice, and it is a snail jump for the daily practice of anything to vaguely regard that practice as a religion.

After all, a lifestyle, whether you are forced to it through poverty or just wander into it on your own, is such an odd way to defend against being fully (painfully) aware of politics cruelties: Americans alas are in groups more than anyone. No doubt some of us are habituated to being in groups. We may even defend them. What's wrong with groups?

Still, at some half-unconscious, fragmented level, some groupies know it would be better to be (a) alone and (b) in the presence of nature. They describe backpacking, even on trails so heartily overused as the John Muir Trail in California, as doing "a spiritual journey." It isn't a spiritual journey: it is enjoying nature. It may even be just a sport. But when we feel oddly anxious, and wish our lives had more meaning than they apparently have, we are prone to inflate the language about what we do—hiking gets called "spiritual journey."

In conclusion: how intelligent people dislike the very mention of "psychological dynamics."

It is human to want any newly discovered truth to come from your own field, not someone else's. Theologians were the gate keepers of the heavens for centuries: they did not greet the arrival of mathematicians in the 17th century with enthusiasm. They responded in the usual two ways by which one can oppose any new insight: first, you pay attention only to the periphery of the inventor's work. People were interested in Copernicus's peripheral work in what we now call astronomy. English and American critics who didn't cotton to Virginia Woolf's anti-war and anti-deprivation-of-women stances praised her for decades for being such a wonderful stylist.

Second, those protecting the old powers that be against change, lie, outright lie, about the new work in order to suppress the public attention it deserves or to utterly subvert its essential meaning. A stunning major (and morally gross) example: Copernicus had more than one man managing his manu-

De Revolutionibus Orbium Coelestium. The last of these was a
Lutheran clergyman, Andreas Osiander, who without getting permission from anyone, attached a Foreword to *De Rev* saying (in
so many words) that one can't really determine such a subject as
the possible movement of earth around a stationary sun, that
Copernicus was not really insisting that the universe is heliocentric, but of course this manuscript has interesting helps to people trying to measure various planets' orbits'. In other words,
Osiander told readers: Copernicus is not really saying that our
universe is heliocentric. At the time, May, 1543, Copernicus may
have already died of his illness. He never saw what the clergyman had done to him by a combination of genial schmooze-
writing and outright lying.

Osiander was afraid. If we read history with the idea of trying to understand how people behave in situations parallel to
contemporary events we know of, we can jeer at one more soft-
spoken Lutheran pastor—that's an easy shot—but Osiander
knew something black Americans and Japanese-Americans of
the Nisei generation knew but which white Americans tend not
to know: Osiander knew what it is to live in an empire. He did
not want his knee caps loosened by the rack. He would not
have wanted to be interrogated at Guantanamo Bay or at Abu
Ghraib.

Another interesting point is the all-too-common lag between
a new major scheme-changing discovery like Copernicus's[15] and
general societal acceptance of it. It was 31 years after the publi-
cation of *De Rev* before anyone made much of Copernicus's
heliocentricity.[16]

In an oddly parallel way dozens and dozens of books after
1945 explored the question of why the German people so fer-
vently followed Adolf Hitler. Nonetheless, professors of the
Kennedy Center for International Affairs in a 1990s talk show
told a television audience verbatim, "Of course no one can pos-

[15] In the 3rd century some Greek philosophers had decided that the world went around the sun,
not the reverse. Copernicus deliberately studied for several years to learn Greek. He had come
across those philosophers' work.
[16] Lawrence M. Principe, *History of Science: Antiquity to 1700*, Part III, "Lecture 26: Copernicus
and Calendrical Reform." The Teaching Company, 4151 Lafayette Center Drive, Suite 100,
Chantilly, VA. www.teach12.com

sibly know why the Germans followed Hitler." Psychology wasn't their field so to those political scientists the work of Bruno Bettelheim, Alice Miller, Robert Jay Lifton, Erik Marcussen, Ervin Staub, and Christopher R. Browning,[17] simply didn't exist. We can think of it this way: during the 31 years after Copernicus announced that the universe goes around the sun, not the earth, any number of university intellectuals kept on meeting in conferences to discuss Ptolemy's ideas as if Copernicus had never lived.

It is hard to find oneself blindsided by new insights. Sister Kenny was out of temper about Dr Salk's vaccine. Dava Sobel's book *Longitude* is the story of how a artisan-class clockmaker solved the problem of determining longitude when at sea, anywhere in the world—but upper class, established astronomers and the like had been studying the moon and stars, doing any amount of math in order to make it possible to tell where you were with respect to east and west. (Latitude—north and south—had not been a problem for centuries.) These privileged upper-class Englishmen hated it that the operative technology was not astronomy but clock-making. They contrived to cheat John Harrison, the clockmaker in question, for decades of his rightful winning of the Longitude Prize £20,000.

Psychology is the perfect case of something of great value that cannot be physically seen. It belongs to the *omnium invisibilium* or Things Invisible of which religious people claim that God is the maker. No matter how eagerly the rest of us urge that psychological dynamics run through and through us, through ourselves and through our groups, there are people who jeer at it with all their will. If they are too well mannered to jeer, they will kid, and if they are too well mannered to kid they will make gentle, unwelcome witticisms.

One very intelligent question heard from psychology-haters, however, is this: "If all this is true, though, where's it going to end?"

The first time I heard that question it was not asked respect-

---

[17] Christopher R. Browning, *Ordinary Men: Reserve police Battalion 101 and the Final Solution in Poland*, New York: HarperCollins, 1992.

fully, but it is an awfully good question. The asker suspects rightly: it *won't* end. Once you accept that dynamic feeling surges or lags, is sped up or is inhibited, surges again, through the rich mantle of the cortex, citing this occasion, urging that theory, rousing that passion, condemning that outmoded instinct, inventing a new theory, there is no end to it. The old stability is gone.

Christa Wolf, a German essayist, wrote, "We have pushed off from the Animal Kingdom forever."[18] No wonder people look balefully on psychology.

The old animal kingdom was much easier.

---

[18] Christina Wolf, *Accident/A Day's News.*

CHAPTER 5

An Elegant Theory of Neuroscience: *Re-Entry*

W hat we honor most of all in a republic and have to protect is minority opinion. What one notices in totalitarian governments, or in governments regressing to totalitarianism, is that minority opinion starts getting regarded as treason. The greatest case of this was Goering's assuring Hitler to go ahead and start the war because once started, all you have to do is get the neighbors of war protesters to turn them in for treason.

Dissenting opinion is protected in our constitution and still confirmed by court cases. The kind of dissenting opinion we would like to discuss in this chapter is the dissenting opinion inside our brains. How is it that the brain of all things, one hundred percent a biological entity, should have a practice by which it repeatedly reminds us and reminds us of minority opinions based on our perceptions of the moment and how they relate to ideas we have formed and saved in the past? It is marvelous. It can be stalled and wasted by culture. It can be enhanced by culture. The potential for constant relating of dissenting and majority opinions *inside ourselves* is there and that potential is there for everybody. A good thing to keep in mind is that just as it is hard to honor minority opinion in a talkative community where everyone else shares the majority opinion, it is hard to honor the *minority opinions inside your brain.* A professor of psychology at the University of California, Berkeley, Charlan Nemeth, urged that we make a point of learning not to revere but "to fear status, power, and majority viewpoints…My own research over the past 20 years [he said] is that minority views, and, in particular, consistent minority dissent are extremely powerful correctives. They stem the likelihood of unreflective conformity."[1]

Professor Nemeth's remarks help us get hold of and hang

---

[1] Professor Charlan Nemeth, "Profiting from Those We Underestimate: Dissent and Innovation," a talk given at the Association of Research Library, May 1996 Membership Meeting Proceedings 128.

onto our own ethics even when they differ from what we read and hear, especially when they differ from what governments announce with so much confidence.[2] If we apply his respect for the minority opinion to the minority opinions inside our own heads we will gratefully welcome an introduction to re-entry.

Of all the work our brains do for us in the way of consciousness the most interesting dynamic is re-entry, or re-entrant thinking. This chapter will attempt to introduce readers to just that one idea of neurobiology.

Before going further, we want to quote the neurologist and author Antonio Damasio because readers have a right to hear from the experts, not just the enthusiastic laypersons who introduce them to what may be an unfamiliar field of knowledge. Please also see the small bibliography at the end of *Stopping the Gallop*. It lists 3 books of Damasio's work. We think they are accessible and philosophically mature and idealistic. Besides, like Lewis Thomas *(Lives of the Cell)*, Damasio is an enchanting essayist.

"Strategies [to cope with the suffering experienced by individuals, whose capacity to remember the past and anticipate the future] could have evolved only in the few species whose brains were structured to permit the following: First, a large capacity to memorize categories of objects and events, and to memorize unique objects and event, that is, to establish dispositional representations of entities and events at the level of categories and at unique level. Second, a large capacity for manipulating the components of those memorized representations and fashioning new creations by means of novel combinations. The most immediately useful variety of those creations consists of imagined scenarios, the anticipation of outcomes of actions, the formulation of future plans, and the design of new goals that can enhance survival. Third,

---

[2] A propos of the confident style so characteristic of those safe in the majority herd, Professor Nemeth quotes Mark Twain's referring to it as the "calm confidence of a Christian with four aces."

a large capacity to memorize the new creations described above…"[3]

Before trying to explain a theory (re-entrant thinking) that we love the principle of but know so very little about, the authors of this book ask our readers to reject two old saws of conventional advice to scholars. Both, like much popular wisdom, serve as kill-joys as we put our minds to work.

The first old saw is the idea that "a little knowledge is a dangerous thing" and the second is that when learning about any new field of knowledge from scratch a person should always start by studying the "building blocks" of whatever that field is rather than its central philosophical principle.

Earlier in this book we have talked about how people who don't think contemplatively get irritable around people who do. When they hear about a new way to inquire into the truth of a subject or to inquire into oneself looking for more profound thinking, they are given to saying, "OK, but let's check out the real world." Popular axioms like "a little knowledge is a dangerous thing" flow like river water from disappointed human beings.[4] Replies to kill-joy remarks need to be slightly sympathetic, however, because having an unthreatened-enough ego so you can get a little knowledge from another discipline is a piece of psychological luck. Of course there is intellectual effort in it: you have to pay attention for a period of time to someone else's ideas, but before you buckle down to such concentration, you had psychological and cultural luck. One workable answer to kill-joy street wisdom is, "You are probably right" and leave it there.

As for the second of the two old saws—the advisory that says you must start by looking very particularly at the building blocks of whatever the new discipline is, that advice fails human beings in two ways: first, looking at raw resources or

---

[3] Antonio Damasio, in *Descartes' Error: Emotion, Reason, and the Human Brain*. New York: G.P. Putnam's Sons (A Grosset/Putnam Book), 1994, on pages 261 and 262.
[4] Note how much popular wisdom just neutralizes the happy spirit of the scholar. "A little knowledge is a dangerous thing."—a remark made to interested laypeople enjoying some knowledge that is new to them. "The more it changes the more it stays the same."—a remark made to psychotherapists by way of telling them their work is ineffective.

tooling up is appropriate to practices, not for the central concept. It is peripheral to the feeling center of that field. To put it coarsely, say you thought you might get interested in one or another religion. You wouldn't read up on chalice metals or how to iron Fair Linen. Those are the equipment, not the affectional center of Anglican Christianity. Even if you wanted to grasp the beauty of a physical wonder, like a medieval church, you wouldn't do a study of medieval masonry. You would contemplate the astounding height of enclosed, very light space, held there under the acute vaulting and all that startling presence of clear glass.

Second, most of us have our lives to live and our livelihood to be made, our families to serve, our government to be monitored—all what is called "having a life." We would never get any grasp at all of re-entry in the human cortex if we started by studying cells, neuron development, neurotransmitters (the chemicals in the brain's synapses) or hormones, the chemicals elsewhere in the brain, gray and white matter makeup in the brain. We'd never get to the central affectional aspect of human brains. If someone puts you off by saying "Then you really haven't the least idea what you are talking about," you can stave them off with "You're probably right" but follow it up with "the good news is that most scientific insights that have brought humanity to one or another new truth about the universe were arrived at intuitively or mathematically long before the innovator had tools to measure the phenomena in question—to wit, Einstein on cosmic theory."

A third behavioral idea clings to the question of how to approach new knowledge. If we look first at the technology of a thing we are doing what children sensibly, logically, do. They figure out *how* to crawl, not *whether* to crawl. Crawling, like all technology, is in itself ethics-neutral. For an adult to spend a lot of time studying other people's work technologies is a pleasant hobby, not ethical inquiry.

Example: one of the most fascinating mechanical successes in the Western world is the medieval invention of tidal mills. We know that they didn't exist in classical times, but medieval inventors had them near Bayonne, in Gascogny, France, and on the Deben Estuary in Suffolk, England. Tidal mills were an ingenious idea for low-lying river mouths where the river's gradient was too slight to give a watermill the head it needs. The tidal mill operator opened his dam gate when the tide came in, the trapped water itself would shut it. The miller would then wait until the difference in water level in his dammed-up pond and the spillwater below was great enough. He opened the gate and made the escaping, falling deluge run his wheel in the millrace. There is always some drawback to any machinery, of course, ingeniously dreamed up or not. Tidal mills could run only just after high tide, and since the tidal schedule changes every day, the miller's work hours had to change, too.[5]

Clearly nothing about that explanation has anything to do with whether people treat each other cruelly or kindly. (No wonder people want to escape into hobbies—as addressed in Chapter 4.)

But ethics doesn't make good parlour games and it won't stay divided into niches like church calendars. Since we are programmed for the potential of altruistic imagination, the brain, or at least some of the brain, is up for the work of moral imagination. The brain, if we are culturally lucky enough to have gotten some formal education, wants to contemplate subjects that do *not* stay discrete from one another. Hence re-entry.

1970s feminist hostility to abstract thinking.

Before actually discussing the cortex's re-entry function we want to argue against one specific bad political movement that has stalled women from being drawn to the modern neurology. One of the strongest ideological forays of the 1970s was one flank of separatist-feminism that made a bugbear of abstract thinking.

Even so late as in the early 1990s one heard feminists saying pejoratively, "That's so abstract!" as if abstract constructs were nothing but a failure to be sensual. That particular pothole of the women's movement—focusing upon and boasting

---

[5] Jean Gimpel, *The Medieval Machine: The Industrial Revolution of the Middle Ages*. First published as *La Revolution Industrielle du Moyen Age* in 1976.

about sensuality—is not a clarion aspect of a movement. Like any movement fighting to get justice and intelligence where there has been injustice and stupidity, the women's movement needed and needs to be as spacious and intelligent as it can be. Demoting the potential of womanly thinking to being principally body-oriented is ironically very anti-women. If body-centeredness lacks intelligence and certainly lacks a holy philosophy, how did it get so much currency?

Some of such thickheadedness benefited by the fact that at the time, not one but two generations of Americans had been watching television. That is to say, millions had diminished their childhood's potential daily reading by three to four hours. Television gives us graphics, not concept.

What had happened and was worsening, it appears, is that thirty years of too few hours spent in re-entry and too many hours spent in graphic sensationalism—Wow! Zapp! Look at that! Slam! There it went! Here's a new scene! Now what are they doing?—that kind of thing is graphics, whether advertising or programming. It is speeded up to make it excite the mind because by then the mind was understimulated intellectually. What had begun and was going apace was the dumbing down of America.

Women wanted to feel confident and capable, however. Of course they did. Who doesn't? What to do? At some inchoate, half-aware level they knew they weren't being very intelligent in rejecting the analytical thinking of forty-thousand years of dead-male thinking. Of course it was unfair that males had bullied women into doing all the childcare and housework so the males got to educate themselves and make theories and philosophies. The unlevel thinking field was unfair, but the fact is, hundreds of males did some good abstract thinking, along with a few women. If woman were going to inveigh against all that intellectual energy of dead white males, they have got to have suspected some loss. Still, they had it on their agenda not to feel unworthy. They wanted to feel worthy *as is*. When people talk about *as is* they usually mean without one's doing any mental work or without needed repairs having been made. The political answer is to lower the common denominator. The common denominator is pleasure life of the body, so those early separatist-feminist went along with the spurious theory that sensual vividness was better than abstract imagination.

Corruption got into it, but not much. A few feminist theorists made a lot of money arguing by flattering one sex at the expense of the other: males, particularly dead white ones, they wrote, may be abstract, linear, and rigid, but we are not. We are vulnerable to each moment's fresh impressions. Somehow they sold this bill of goods. Shakespeare, then, got pointed to as a loser, with his philosophical genius, his wonderful tying of details to theory. In fact, there are still 1970s feminist English teachers who have not read *Hamlet* and they don't intend to. They negatively condition their students to reading Shakespeare. Amazing. That they are still around, barbed-wire fencing the young away from the geniuses of culture speaks to the strength of l970s anti-intellectualism in women.

Another bill of goods was a spurious idea: that women learn in groups whereas males learn in solitude. Unfortunately great art and great philosophy and a good deal of other culture is made only in solitude by either men or women. Groups are all right for what is called "support" and also for social justice. The work done by Restorative Justice groups is wonderful. But you can't write or devise formulae or envision new systems if you are sitting in a group. Women wasted young women's time by advising them to get into groups to do work that can only be done alone. This was a disservice to those young women.

Gerald M. Edelman wrote that he did some bashing of other neurologists' theories lest readers come across them and be misled. I was happy to read that Edelman deliberately criticized what he regarded as mistaken theories. It saves me a tremendous amount of time not to read through out-of-date theories that haven't held up to scrutiny. With Edelman's frankness in mind, I have printed the above objections to anti-intellectualism in women. We will save time if we use our heads as profoundly as we can.

We would be mad to settle for mere sense impressionability when we could be taking heart from our own brains' work in uniting and strengthening our own philosophies of life.

Re-entry theory

The higher-level consciousness of homo sapiens is one of the wondrous aspects of our brains, but because this is a book about learning how to live—and vote—from the most deeply held feelings of our brains, let's look not at consciousness generally, but at a single dynamic of the neocortex called re-entry. It is the process that best demonstrates to us why we have so very many evaluative feelings and so very many impulses to categorize and theorize and work out our species's amazing love of "getting it together," "tying things up," "sorting it out"— in a word, having a unified personal philosophy that belongs to this one creature only—myself.

The modern neurological hypothesis called re-entry is that when a perception goes in one of our senses, say, our eyes, a message goes to the cortex. The message says, "Here is something new" or "Here is something we have seen before, haven't we?" The message is carried to various neurons and neuron groups in the cortex. Like an old-fashioned Western Union boy, the message always waits for a reply. It brings replies back from the various places he delivered the message. A key point of re-entry: the reply goes back not only to the sender but reciprocally to all the other receivers. The reply is accumulative and communal: the reply says, "Yes, Eyes, you did see something new," or it says, "No, Eyes, we've seen that before," and it says: "About that message you sent, Eyes, some of us are in favor, some are against, some are fascinated, some of us don't give a damn about it, some of us are terrified, which is why, if you will look down at your body, you will notice that just now you have done a u-turn and the legs are running as fast as they can. Some of us think that what you just saw changes everything—Oh, everything! Everything for the worse! Or everything for the better! Curse you, Eyes! Or, thank you, Eyes." Those are typical replies.

Re-entry theory as clearing up mistaken ideas about the "self."

We will now add another reason to be glad of this particular neurological theory. It is that this one aspect of the latest neurology, re-entry, lets us quite easily substitute truth for some of the folk wisdoms floating around that are not truth. Lies unfortunately do prevail unless empirically supported science cuts through them. In terms of re-entrance theory: here are two lies of folk wisdom about the brain, lies of long standing and some cultural éclat, too.

A lie: that any fleeting feeling one has in response to some sensory perception is shallow or it wouldn't be fleeting and you would have remembered it.

A second lie: that deep inside our brain is a single, vaguely identified real self with its steady, ongoing, basically unchanged real feelings. People instinctively suppose that this "real self" is singular whereas the various fleeting intuitions or hypotheses that flare up and vanish, light up again and again vanish, in our consciousness, are plural. We tend to think of this projected singular, real, self of ours as being in opposition to a number of shallow "received ideas" —that is, opinions we accepted and picked up from the culture, or had dredged into us like flour into meat by big people with authority over us—our parents, our Fuehrer, our school principal, our retro and overly directive pastor, or an oligarchy of power freaks called "The Faculty" at whatever school or college we attended.

And a third lie: that somehow or other, without our really doing much about it except reading some texts someone pointed us to—if we could just get the time—our brain will steady onto what we think of as "its true course" or "the true course of our reliably static personality," and "well—that'll be more or less it, for us. It'll work out, see, when we get the time."

This sounds like mere drifting, but actually bodes worse than mere sloth. Likely what lies under this particular untrue statement is the primitive, deterministic assumption that people come in various types: fate, therefore, should we live so long, will just naturally solidify us as the type of person that "we were always meant to be." All notions colored by such fatalism are infinitely comfortable to people who don't want to gather themselves for any of the higher barrier-jumps in the steeple chase of life. That is, fate lays the soft mantle of hopelessness-of-change over everything. Fatalism loosens people's resolve so that an unpleasant further effect of it is that fatalists are subject to great loneliness: they don't want to feel both without any personal say in life and without hope of changing anything, so they tend to herd together. They are attracted to aphorisms: Life is this way. Life has always been this way. That's life for you, every time! And so forth. Kill-joy aphorisms, usually uttered in a jocular, good-sport tone, aren't the most cheerful conversation, but they work perfectly for herd communication. They do not threaten anybody with anything fresh or different.

Sociologists and anthropologists not very surprisingly tell us that the more primitive a given human culture, the more group-oriented it is. As for groups themselves, a group in which either people are afraid to distance themselves from the others inside the group or people have failed to imagine for themselves, privately, some outcomes they should have been thinking about, would be, say, a controlling group that loves only the mediocre. That would be a group that would have preferred Virginia's House of Burgesses without its Patrick Henry, or the Justice Department without Oliver Wendell Holmes, or the field of environmental sciences without Rachel Carson, or the practice of military nursing without its Florence Nightingale.

Anything that comes naturally, such as clinging to the com-mon-denominator opinion of groups or feeling that fate decides everything has been with us a lot longer than any phi-losophy that civilization has actually had to teach its young. This is what makes peaceable and democratic civilization so fragile.

When I lived on a farm I sometimes did chores for a neigh-boring farm family so they could go on vacation. I learned that pigs, under stress, revert to wild boar-like ancestry much faster than any other farm animals. I was surprised. Pigs and cats are more intelligent than the more affectionate horses and dogs. So why are they vulnerable to going retro? And human beings—a thousand times more analytical and memory-based than even pigs and cats—who have used re-entrant work in their elegant cortices to develop republics, laws, respect for individually superior leaders[6]—why of all things would they—we—be vulnerable to falling back into primitive group behaviors?

A two-part speculation: first, civilization is not yet gene-specified. Civilization still has to be learnt by each organism from its mentors. And second, human beings teach civilization to only *some* of their young.

Any procedure or philosophy that has to be verbally taught to the young gets taught to very few young first, only later to the less privileged people's young. We bring this up because of the time lag between the time when a few have been taught some rather exquisite principle or use and the time when those lower in the class system are allowed to participate.[7] Although "Don't stereotype people!" has been a politically correct shout for a few decades, the majority of Europeans and Americans have never heard of the idea of how people grow in cognition, sentience, and altruism through stages that have been identified severally by Erik Erikson, Lawrence Kohlberg, and Jane Loevinger among others.[8]

Supposing people to come in types is of such long standing that it seems quite respectable. Unless a keen stage-development person wanders into your neighborhood, you understandably might all your life see people as more or less static

---

[6] Stephen Jay Gould gave human beings a great shaking up when he pointed out that evolution doesn't go slowly and gradually: some special event drives it forward, and individuals with superior intelligence, it would seem, who cogitate inside their own brains instead of knuckling under to the tribal chieftain, think up solutions and save the day for anyone who will follow them. They have to watch their backs, because history is full of chieftains who felt threatened by these innovative types and either ostracized or killed them.

[7] In our pig of a species, the lag is not an accident. If you are a person who has been allowed to gratify your enjoyment of bullying people, then to deprive some wonderful experience or even necessities in life to others—because you have the position and power to do it—it would be hard not to give yourself this evil pleasure. Christian IV of Denmark admired the figured socks that Danish poor women knitted, usually while ambling along watching the sheep. In 1636 he forbade any wives to wear whole socks. Men could, but women had to wear just their wooden shoes with some ankle- and leg warmers above. There was no possible reason for such an edict except that it made fun for the King. It was natural fun, perhaps an evolutionary step or two away from the fun of a cat's torturing a bitten, safely controlled mouse.

[8] We haven't any information about Asian or African familiarity with moral stage-development theory.

types. Once one has a look at how an open-minded brain changes as it functions, becomes more various and much deeper as it tries to sort conflicting data and conflicting philosophies, it seems preposterous that anyone could believe people are certain types. We have to forgive ourselves, though, and remember that untrue ideas, once they get going, wash up and cling onto small minds like sea wrack. Lies don't even weaken or die naturally: lies actually have to be shouted down flat by individual people taking the trouble to shout, "That's never been true and it isn't true now!" and so forth. Any of us can tot up a short list of bad ideas that lasted for eons: slavery, for example, is natural and it is all right. Not letting ignorant people vote is natural, and it is all right. The universe is earth-centered, not heliocentric.

It is pleasant to think of all the unjust theories that have been exposed as lies. It is pleasant to list a few human beings who have exposed a lot of lies just in the last twenty-five years. Seymour Hersh, Molly Ivins, Lewis Thomas, Lewis Lapham, Barbara Ehrenreich.

Denise Levertov was right in her poem, "Modulations," to rejoice in "the luxury of unlearning old lies."[9]

To use parallels—metaphors—to describe re-entry theory of the neocortex in the simplest way: once the senses have sent a perception in to the brain, the brain sends that news around via its chemo-electric moving dynamic core of neurons. They touch one another by the hundreds of thousands.[10]

Everything is done by a process we traditionally call "memory."

The term "memory" is a little blousy because throughout investigations into the brain it has meant so many different

---

[9] Please see in the Appendix a copy of one stanza of this outstanding poem. In the year before her death I asked Denise Levertov for permission to use this one (final) stanza of her poem called "Modulations." I wouldn't have thought of it, she said—but yes. Good idea. She looked surprised. I don't think she realized even then that the rest of a principally narrative poem was all right but that this stanza was brilliant.

[10] A neuron's presynaptic synapse does not actually touch the postsynaptic synapse of the next neuron: the message is sent chemically across the gap. A rough parallel is how ions leave a pole in a battery to travel across to the opposite.

things. Still, it is the term we have. When neurons in our cortexes are conferring about something we sense this minute, other neurons are functioning in the way they function when checking out past events and past concepts in our heads. It helps to think of the brain being in touch with its own far reaches the way a large ship is in touch with itself: neurons all over the six laminated layers of the cortex and some in the brain's older, more body-oriented, less concept-oriented nuclei deep inside or immediately below the mantle of cortex, get sent word of some new perception. They reply "New perception, ay ay," or "Old idea being reevaluated, ay ay" as a dynamic core of selected neurons makes its report.

A word about the non-conscious work of the brain: neurons alert and competent at their posts in the cerebellum, the brain stem, in the other regions outside of what is called the thalamocortical system are doing non-conscious work. These neurons are not interested in love.

I will explain that fatuous remark. Conscious work of the brain is what urges our species, and perhaps other higher mammals' families as well, toward familiarity with more of the universe than mere survival would deem necessary. More familiarity breeds more affection for the universe, however we experience it. Or, as in the case of vicarious experience, however we may wish we experienced it. We read books, for example—poetry and novels—in order to experience, and get a kick from, not just our own lives but from other people's lives. The philosopher Ludwig Wittgenstein reminded us that fish do not make clear statements about salinity in seawater. Fish haven't got our six-layers of upper cortex and they don't do "higher consciousness." We do. We are interested not only in our element, air, but also in other elements. Lucky kids get read aloud stories by adults in which animals and fish speak and have desires and specific fears. Children then imagine those desires and fears. That's conscious work that their minds love to do. It is majestic work, too.

We say this because so much current babble about the brain makes a fetish of unconsciousness as if it had a spiritual value of some sort. What unconsciousness has is utter practicality—it is nature at work, connecting head to muscles so we can act. Returning some impulse from the muscles, as well. "All is not well down here," the muscles may send, to the conscious cortex: "Stop the work order, please. It is not OK down here."[11]

C.G. Jung wrote several passages about people brought to him because recurring dreams had left them feeling anxious or terrified Jung identified the dreams as the body warning the upper ranges of the brain that death was breeding elsewhere in the organism.[12] The body sent its desperate news. Those amazing, still seemingly mystifying messages from the amygdala or other brain entry spots receiving news from the body are life-preserving communication, so far as we, the organism, are concerned. Such news is not holy work, however touching. Holy work is done in the imagination—the re-entry—of the cortex and has to do with imagining how it might be better for others, how shall we make it better, what could we try.

Re-entry process lets us sort out the comparative value of various thoughts we have: those that are superficial association, those that rouse body terrors, those that create new ideas in our minds. A one-sentence poem by William Carlos Williams below is followed by an essay about reading that poem re-entrantly.

Here's the scene. We have decided to read a poem, for whatever reason. Our eyes are on the page in good faith. The brain's neurons, in their millions, are doing their part in good faith. They are gathering associations that we have previously "remembered"—or they are remembering only this minute right now because of the poem.

Any poem worth two cents brings up all sorts of conflicting judgments in the mind. Psychologists and neuroscientists use

---

[11] Re-entry, that is, reciprocal messaging between perceptive sites and other parts of the brain, and among other sites of the brain and one another, is a feature primarily of the cortex. It is related to our consciousness. It helps to keep in mind that some messages are both received and forwarded by non-conscious neurons in our brains as well. Their jobs are not making useful concept out of a mix of perception and already-held values the way the cortex does. Their work is monitoring and maintaining the conditions of the organism (that's us) as well as they can. We wouldn't want to be conscious of their days' and nights' work even if we could be.
[12] Carl Gustav Jung, *Memories, Dreams, Reflections*.

that odd term, *qualia*, which we understand to mean perceptions and concepts that we have a lot of feeling about while we think. Our brains have made a category for one quale or another, the way one would save shelf space for a valued object. Each quale, we suppose, has a feeling value of some sort for us or the neurons wouldn't fire it up. Good poems, however, bring up qualia that don't agree with one another. We like poetry if we like its irony between apparently conflicting qualia. You know the expression "I am of two minds about it."

What re-entry theory suggests is that from our brain's point of view, what looks superficially like contradictions may well be not only sound but profoundly felt. You have heard the expression, "Yes, yes, I know...but somehow I also feel that..." The speaker may feel 6 or 1000 values (feelings), all of which are sound and sincere, neurons firing all over the cortex saying, "Here's what I think, hey!" Other neurons saying: "Please—you, the organism, the one that runs this place—if you're the one running this place, would you listen? Is there anyone running this place? For God's sake, would you listen? Because here's what I think!'

Here is William Carlos Williams's poem in its entirety.

So much depends
upon

a red wheel
barrow

glazed with rain
water

beside the white
chickens.

Here is an essay written about reading the poem while thinking about the re-entrant style of the cortex.

"Why read poetry?"[13]

Poetry does all the good things we say it does. It deepens our feeling, it sharpens our ideas. It shows us the fine points of things. All that is true.

But now there is good news from biologists—a new way to describe how poetry changes the brain. And what is the brain? In addition to its marvelous nuclei, thalamus, hippocampus and stem and all the other chemo-electric underbrush, all strung with blood and finely slung—in addition to all that, six layers lie like a soft cloth in crevasses and wrinkled mountains just under our skulls. These are the six-way cortex. When a new sight or sound—or a poem—comes in, all six layers, billions of individual neurons fire, wink out again, refire, relaying their various takes on the new sight or sound or poem. "Look, look!" the ocular nerve says, because we are sitting in a chair reading: "So much depends upon a red wheel barrow glazed with rain water beside the white chickens." (William Carlos Williams's celebrated poem). The news whips around the 10-to-the-30th-power neurons. "Hey! one part of the cortex agrees: a lot depends on the red wheelbarrow and all"—but another part of the cortex says, "So? An outmoded luggage carrier painted red? What else is new?" Another part, from deeper in the brain where warnings and safety instruction come from, mutters, "Red! Don't talk 'red'! Blood is red, and when there's blood, you're talking dangerous!" And another part, a part of the brain that picks up on shallow fragments of association and forgets a good deal of every conversation and its own diary entries as well—a part of the brain that informs a good deal of human conversation, alas—says, "Red! We kids begged Mom! We told her! She doesn't look good in red—but would she listen? Not her! Those god-awful suits!"

The brain re-entries all over its upper circuitry the news of the red wheelbarrow. It takes approximately 3 seconds.

[13] Hungry Mind Book Store ran a contest in Fodder for essays entitled "Why Read Poetry?" This one won Honorable Mention and $25 certificate for books.

(Gerald Edelman, in *Bright Air, Brilliant Fire*). And what has all this to do with poetry?

Let us imagine the world without poetry. We would just be practical people. "Red wheelbarrow," we would say. We wouldn't speak in a jeering tone—practical people don't jeer so much as they'd like to because in a groupy culture like the United States you lose useful business contacts if you jeer. We would say, "That's OK if you can't make payments on a car." Or we would settle for our scattershot anecdotes—how we scorn our mothers' clothes. Our mind would skimp along on its low-gauge wiring, pausing here and there among its listless insights. In a world without poetry we'd have heard of that short poem by William Carlos Williams, but "Seen one set of leghorns seen 'em all," we would explain. "That goes for wheelbarrows, actually, since you mention it."

As to the mental practice of praising:

In a world without poetry we would not spend much time praising anything. Praisefulness is a taste acquired by people who have been either educated in the liberal arts or mentored. Merely practical people seldom bother with praising the particulars of anything. No one suggested they praise, so they don't. Praising things for their humor, goodness, or beauty is a behavior somewhat more profound than saying Please and Thank you. Like saying please and thank you, however, praise is a cultural, not a genetic or "natural" behavior, so it has to be taught us.

So poetry, which is always on about something either aesthetic or moral, says: "You can kid and jeer all you like. If someone says, 'I love God,' go ahead and tell them to 'Lighten up.' Or otherwise," poetry says quietly, "You do a little climb on the moral stage-development ladder. You could shut up the jeering. You could shut up and let thought glimmer throughout the branches of your own brain's strange thickets, where every tree touched makes more trees to touch."

Poetry says, "Even if you are broke, and have low self-esteem, if Republicans are vicious and Democrats are slug-a-beds, poetry invites you to fly on the fast lightning in your mind—so much depends on the circuits in your head."

It helps to take in this notion and then not allow it to vanish from your mind: the brain is mad keen on loving life. It wants to do it. Mad as it sounds it is true. The brain wants to love life.

We all know the dismal but practical expression "the writing process." It means practicing trust in the re-entrant qualities of one's mind.

By paying attention, the author picks up on the fact that some neurons say shallow things and more and more neurons, if the writer is paying attention, say deeper and deeper things. One stops saying that everything is sociological, for instance, when really, much of life is about psychology and holiness. This process accounts for the philos (Greek for love) of the word philosophy.

Let us use one more ingenious work of literature that is almost precisely about re-entrance among our brains' cortices: it is two passages from Wordsworth's amazing "Preface to the Lyrical Ballads, Second edition," of 1800—nearly two hundred years before Gerald Edelman used the word "re-entry." Wordsworth is talking about that process of taking a sensed perception, weighing it inside yourself, giving it a definite value. A value, in the brain—and this is Antonio Damasio[14]—is a category made with feeling. Damasio emphatically and very clearly distinguishes between emotions, which are primary reactions to things, reactions that we can't order not to have—such as terror—and feelings, which are evaluations made in our cortex.

Here is Wordsworth, from his "Preface to Lyrical Ballads, Second Edition, 1800"

> "For the human mind is capable of being excited without the application of gross and violent stimulants; and he must have a very faint perception of its beauty and dignity who does not know this, and who does not further know that one being is elevated above another in proportion as he possesses this

---

[14] Especially in Damasio's *The Feeling of What Happens* and *Looking for Spinoza*. See the bibliography in the Appendix.

capability. It has therefore appeared to me that to endeavor to produce or enlarge this capability is one of the best services in which, at any period, a writer can be engaged; but this service, excellent at all times, is especially so at the present day. For a multitude of causes, unknown to former times, are now acting with a combined force to blunt the discriminating powers of the mind, and, unfitting it for all voluntary exertion, to reduce it to a state of almost savage torpor. The most effective of these causes are the great national events which are daily taking place, and the increasing accumulation of men in cities, where the uniformity of their occupations produces a craving for extraordinary incident, which the rapid communication of intelligence hourly gratifies. ...I think upon this degrading thirst after outrageous stimulation..."

Wordsworth supposed that people who practiced a good deal of what we would call re-entry were a different type of person from those who didn't. (We now know that the scope and elegance with which you practice re-entry is a cultural blessing or curse, not a measure of character traits.) Wordsworth, however, lived well before people knew about any cognitive stage-development theory, and you don't make your judgments on the basis of developmental philosophies unless you were taught them. So he naturally praised himself, farther into the Preface, for doing so much imaginative work inside himself—for being impervious to the lust for violence and sensation that non-inner people are prey to.

"...For all good poetry is the spontaneous overflow of powerful feelings: and though this be true, poems to which any values can be attached were never produced on any variety of subjects but by a man who, being possessed of more than usual organic sensibility, had also thought long and deeply. For our continued influxes of feeling are modified and directed by our thoughts, which are indeed the representatives of all our past feelings: and, as by contemplating the relation of these general representatives to each other, we discover what is really important to men so, by the repetition and continuance of this act, our feelings will be connected with important subjects, till at length, if we be originally possessed of much sensibility, such habits of mind will be produced that, by obeying blindly and mechanically the impulses of those habits, we shall describe objects, and utter sentiments of such a nature, and in such connection with each other, that the understanding of the reader must necessarily be in some degree enlightened, and his affections strengthened and purified."

If Wordsworth, immediately above, is right about how reading the thoughts of people who have practiced re-entry will in turn strengthen and purify our affections, then likely we need to think, in 2004, that if we don't read any work by people who rely on not just their sense impressions but upon their cortex's connections between all such perceptions and all past thinking, our "affections" as he puts it above, will be weaker and less pure. This gives us a neurobiologically advised way to understand the cynical flip of post-modernism. Gone with the habit of solitude and contemplation is the philo of philosophy—a general affection.

It is wonderful to see how deliberately deciding to stay conscious of one's own re-entrant process invites one to the serious, total awareness of one's various few million niches in the cortex. Lewis Thomas, the scientist and essayist, noted about basic research that you conduct it in an atmosphere of collegiality and likely failure and humor.[15] That's parallel to trusting the re-entrant process.

An unasked-for preachment[16] about trusting our own re-entry, then:

1. Say we just saw a horror of low, middle, or high intensity: we must trust that our eyes did not deceive us.

2. Next we should trust that our thalamocortical neurons have relayed their firing to all sorts of brain settings, connecting some earlier learned concepts about similar or dissimilar horrors.

3. Now perhaps our mind is presenting us with 19 different messages about that horror we just saw, only one of which messages keeps saying, "Look, you could have a go at turning this thing around—you could, yes, *you*." If we trust in this fascinating aspect of re-entry, chances are this minority voice of ours, the "one out of the nineteen," is more summoning than all the others put together.

---

[15] Lewis Thomas, *Lives of the Cell*.

[16] Notice how terrified education and psychology groupies are of "being preachy!" They must suppress a human longing to be preachy. In fact, preaching is an old cultural artifact. Look how at Thanksgiving dinner the pater familias won't let go the imprisoned hands he has hold of on either side of himself. The huge bird is cooling but he won't stop talking. He is preaching. He doesn't care if everyone else is a starved atheist. He wants to preach and he keeps doing it. There is nothing so bull-headed as someone determined to preach. So we let go and did a preachment on opening your mind to respecting its own reentry potential.

CHAPTER 6

In the Presence of our Enemies

Thou preparest a table before me in the presence of mine enemies.
—Psalm 23:5

E very given creature has a set of enemies, physical or psychological. We even keep old past enemies in mind, because long ago the brain "internalized" them. When entities get internalized, if it is done unconsciously, they can weaken one's free-hearted thinking; that is, someone dominated our opinions way back and we keep on feeling that those particular opinions are wrong, or we lose trust in many other of our opinions. When old enemies are internalized and somehow nourished unrealistically, then we may behave in a paranoid, fashion— that is, to take offense in the present where no offense is meant just because something about today's scene reminded us of the old huge offensive scene of the past. Finally, some people diligently keep memories of old enemies alive. They aren't necessarily neurotic. They are probably just people who enjoy a grudging temper.

Not only must every creature somehow manage its enemies but every new idea pattern inside the human brain—inside each of our own brains—will have its enemies right there in the brain. The enemies will be such old ideas or perhaps incoming ideas from today's culture on the outside which have everything to lose if we befriend a new philosophy inside ourselves.

Here is a common kind of thought-enemy that family members all over the world and reformers in any community will recognize: whenever a creature decides to upgrade its own behavior it picks up a little coterie of enemies it had casually taken for friends.

About the bizarre notion of having our table prepared for us in the presence of our enemies: Let me straightaway make an accusation against the brand of comfortable group philosophies that started with the "greening of America" in 1965 but are a huge societal influence now. Typical American group philosophy resists bringing mention of enemies into all questions of philosophy and personality growth. Of course people prefer blissful ideas to ideas full of dread. They want all ethical projects to be a matter of self-development—of freeing one oneself from old thought habits, or telling oneself how related all things in the universe are. Nothing to do with enemies. Gaia, for example, the philosophical idea of nature all being a single organism with variety but not enmity in its membership, is one of the most cheerful ideas in the world. It relieves stress to carry around comfortable ideas like that. It is no accident, we should bear in mind, that since the 1960s one of the key words of community organizers has been "comfortable." American mid-level idealists would like to be comfortable as they confer.

Comfort-lovers are not true friends to the little creatures of the world. They are willing to meditate with and mentor little creatures, to help them feel more comfort by seeing how connected we all are. Gorgeous thought. A mouse had rather you drove off Kitty, however. The trouble with that silky feeling how connected we all are is that it gives a free hand to low-paying corporations and unscrupulous-acting governments. When intellectual rhetorical religionists and casual intellectuals do nothing but offer comfortable philosophies to the great and the small, then who is left to point out that the wolf really is a wolf and it has a wolf's mission, just as a cat has its specific mission with respect to mice. Corporate and government forces know how first to negotiate with the weak, and second, how to starve them in order to move what used to be their sustenance over to their own vaults. I think the writer of psalm 23 who put in that odd line about having our table prepared in the presence of our enemies knew something that people sitting on patios and in pews and in courtrooms need to remember. *The opposition is real.*

Anecdotes make poor evidence for science, but if the author isn't lying they have this virtue: they give us a story and vivid picture. Here are three that illustrate how quietly rises right before us the opposition to any idealistic project we have in hand. Our opponents are not ghosts. As often as not they are those we love, and will go on loving, too. But they oppose our deepest interests.

My aunt's no-nonsense distaste for any hallmarks of Christianity

During the time of what was called the Charismatic Renewal in many Christian churches, around 1965 to 1970, I briefly enjoyed that oddball happiness of converts. I call it oddball because even then I didn't feel perfectly respectful of the charismatic renewal. There always seemed to be some liars hanging about. I felt scorn for its artlessness, too. Blithe over-confidence is endemic with converts. Only a month ago, I was building sand-and-twig-and-stolen-gravel garages in a Minneapolis park with my grandson. A youngish woman with a child paused with the broad smile of the kind of extrovert who likes everyone. Teddy and I were carefully putting sand onto the garage roofs so that his tiny light-brown-painted back hoe would be protected from all weathers, but I was civil when the woman spoke. I agreed it was a wonderful day, breeze moving the leaves above the children's play. "Thanks be to the Lord," she then exclaimed, smiling with her huge teeth designed to bite through agnostics—"Thanks be to the Lord!" she repeated. She then added, "There's pretty much not anything He can't handle!" I felt the indignation you feel when you're being shoved to see how much land you'll give up. I felt that the Lord was not handling the cutting of public school funding at all. Converts expect you to return their smiles. They don't expect to be told, "I'm on the other side, actually."

I prefer the neurologist Gerald M. Edelman's attitude: if people are going at some serious activity (in his case, neurology) and they are mistaken, someone must stop it or instead of learning from one another we will be flooded with false doctrines.

> "No one likes to spend much time being critical when there is creative work to do. But in order to explain why the kind of biological theory put forth in this book [*Bright Air, Brilliant Fire*] is needed, I have to do a bit of bashing—to criticize several received ideas and established points of view."[1]

---

[1] Gerald M. Edelman, the opening passage of "Mind Without Biology: A Critical Postscript," in *Bright Air, Brilliant Fire: On the Matter of the Mind*, New York: Basic Books, 1992, 211.

The Charismatic Renewal had its appalling disciples, as any movement has. Those who annoyed me the most were white males and females who kept publicly thanking Jesus for helping them raise their sales levels. A marker of these young-business-oriented Christians was that they affected Southern accents when praying or preaching. Somehow, in 1967 and 1968, you didn't sound like a real Christian unless you had that Southern drawl. I used to be able to spot it fairly accurately—it was a kind of cross between a USA Southern accent and the drawl that early astronauts affected when talking to Houston Control. Of course there were genuine Southern accents, because there were Southern charismatic Christians, but what one noticed was the fake ones. I knew my patience with that kind of self-absorbed and posturing and boasting Christianity would be short, but I hungrily learned something from that movement: some things are holy, I learned, and if you are lucky tears come to your eyes in the presence of something holy. How stupid this sounds! —but look at how people do *not* feel the holiness around them and wish for it. Half of the feeling Wordsworth described in his Preface to the Lyrical Ballads, Second Edition[2] really comes of his sense of the holy. People, thousands of people, would like to have that sense of the holy. They bravely join earnest study groups or they undertake spiritual journeys. Usually the studies and the journeys don't yield much holiness: the study groups remain earnest, very polite study groups and the spiritual journeys remain beautiful backpacking trips up the steep slopes of Nepal and Bhutan.

Christian charismatics in the United States of 1965 thanked Jesus for answering their prayers for job success and surviving dull marriages while Robert Jay Lifton, Primo Levy, Bruno Bettelheim, and Elie Wiesel were trying to teach Westerners as clearly as they could about what the Nazis did to Slavs, Jews, Jehovah's Witness, Gypsies, and millions of others. Those wise authors begged Americans to take Nazi psychology seriously because group psychoses or criminal addiction are not nation-specific. Psychology is not nation-specific. If the Nazis got satisfaction from torture and genocide, others had done so before them, and

---

[2] See the discussion of Wordsworth and also the passages quoted in Chapter 5.

others in other continents might get a penchant for torture or genocide *after* them.

All that was very bad news, of course, but I happened to be reading it up at the same time as I received the gift of falling into tears when opening the Bible anywhere. The suffusion of tears, the exploding love that the human heart gets into sometimes, was lovely but my career as a charismatic Christian was doomed. I would ask at the so-called "Power Prayer Meetings" whether any of those people at Dachau or Auschwitz had prayed to God and if so, did He respond, and if He responded, why did He respond by allowing the Nazis to gas 6.5 million people? A few study prayer-meeting members brazened it out, of course. The Roman Catholics generally by repeating their sturdy adage about God and the church, too, being mysterious, period, and the Protestants, but only a few, by saying those victims must have sinned in some terrible way. The other pray-ers held their peace. They had had hopes of this group that met so democratically on Wednesday evenings. Everyone was very kind and the word "love" and a genuine feeling of love flowed around us. Then some sorehead brought up that sorehead stuff about Germany.

I didn't last long as a charismatic Christian. Still, inspiration is inspiration, and for many months I would open the Bible nearly anywhere[3] and be moved to tears.

Summer came. I drove my young children from our farm in western Minnesota to visit an ageing aunt in Duluth. Genevieve convened a family gathering for afternoon coffee and sherry. One of the guests was my cousin in the State Department, an impressive man. He had been stationed in Teheran, but when the United States decided to join with the Shah, my cousin asked to be posted. Other family members, Genevieve's younger sister among them, my father and one or two brothers, sat in front of Genevieve's fire. We let her draw us all out, leading the conversa-

---

[3] The book of Numbers and the book of Leviticus are the two OT books that even Charismatic Christians admitted to "not getting a blessing from." Getting a blessing was Charismatic Renewal language for feeling one's soul shudder, literally, and one's eyes fill with tears upon reading one or another passage in the Bible. The book of Leviticus, especially, has been the basis for anti-literalist jokes on the internet. One of these purported to be a letter to a Christian Coalition mentor asking if, as the letter writer was a new convert, instead of himself stoning his neighbor to death as commanded in Leviticus would it be OK to call 911 and ask the police to do it.

tion in a crisp, genuinely interested way as she had done for over a half-century. At no point in the afternoon did I say "By the way, Genevieve, my eyes fill with tears when I open the Bible," but I must have mentioned the Bible. Converts to anything have an appalling egotistical urge to hint at their excitement even if they have the decency not to make annoying self-revelations. That is no doubt part of why people's spirits sink upon finding a convert in the room.

Genevieve had been knitting. She was like the aunts in Dickens: they knit delicate, pale blue, petal-pink, sunlight-yellow woolens for great-nephews and great-nieces. Now she lay down her knitting and called across the circle in her clarion voice, "It seems to me," she said, "We're hearing a lot about the Bible all of a sudden! Would you mind explaining why?"

The courteous little circle of men and women perked up. An extended-family quarrel started by an elderly *tante terrible* is a freshet on the soil of any three-generation coffee party.

I realized then that I had forgotten that Genevieve was one of six siblings brought up as game agnostics, both of whose parents bade their children think for themselves. When they died what they went to was their biological deaths. While they lived, no one in that family took as authority any experts except Plato and Shakespeare. Plato and Shakespeare make the cut as OK authorities in even the most free-thinking, liberal-arts-educated families. Plato and Shakespeare are the assigned heroes of sometime English majors. That whole family tended to mention their names from time to time, and at least three of them so far as I know, one dead attorney, one dead author, and my state-department cousin present this afternoon, had read them contemplatively. The Bible, however, was very liber non gratus. The family took the Hebrew Old Testament for an excellent window into a horribly nationalistic and violent record of male land acquisition and the New Testament for being slightly crazed. So Genevieve asked me, "Why are we hearing all this mention of the Bible?"

I then realized that I needed to defend myself at some level. So I said "Sorry, Genevieve, I can't help you with that!" Like other people inexperienced but willing to defend themselves I wanted to be as forthright and rude as possible.

Later the state-department cousin said to me "That was just the right thing to say. Good for you!" —whereupon a new strange idea lit up clear in my brain: anyone upgrading their feelings (which is how the brain categorizes its evaluations) will notice some surprising close enemies to the upgrade. Well, any alcoholic proposing to become a recovering alcoholic knows that the other family drinkers rouse up some scorn to oppose them. The idea was new to me.

It was my first *consciousness* that if any member of any tribal group decides to intensify his or her engagement with life the other members may put up some opposition. They may continue to be your loved and loyal relations, but they are unmistakably inimical to your upgrading your inner life.

Second example of being heedless of enemies: The National Farmers Union

I was one of a four-person team of "humanities leaders" hired by the National Farmers Union. The National Endowment for the Humanities paid our project to teach philosophy and literature to young farm couples, the NFU idea being that learning that there even *was* such a thing as high-minded ethical thinking, and then trying to make your own decisions on the basis of ideal *rightness* as well as habitual rural practicality would make good leadership training.

One night our boss, the vice-president of the National Farmers Union, Victor Ray, who had visited our presentations all that day, bawled out us humanities consultants. Victor was very direct with us. He said that if the fur didn't fly we weren't really doing ethics. Someone, he said, always stands to gain by how the place is being run *now* and whoever those people are they are going to oppose your reforms unless they are fools.

I was shocked but delighted, because I had been feeling cloyed in our little clique of right-thinking humanities teachers. No one would say anything unfriendly about anyone. We were always discussing whether or not to do contour plowing, but no one would warn our young farm couples about the scorn thrown at the first contour plowers. Victor Ray waked me up to a tough psychological truth that any business person could have told me if I had only known one. Evil, Victor taught me, if you find it around you, is caused by people who benefit from it.

Hamlin Garland,[4] the wonderful rural moralist and egalitarian whose stories and memoir vividly described farming in the last half of the nineteenth century, is always remembered as someone who did just that: vividly described farming in the last half of the nineteenth century. He also loudly shouted that if farmers and farmers' wives bent their backs in such harsh labor until in old age they could no longer straighten them and still were poor it was not "just the nature of farming." It was the nature of an unnecessarily cruel economy with prices locked in by self-serving rich people. It is curious how people have read Garland but mysteriously *forget* his ethic. The boarding school I attended assigned *A Son of the Middle Border* to us because it was such a vivid picture of agriculture long past. No one told us Garland was a high-minded change agent.

So it is our habit to grow up without even seeing that justice and mercy have enemies and those enemies may be seated very close to us. Victor Ray wanted young National Farmers Union members to break the habit of blithe unconsciousness, but first the poor fellow had to break the habit in the four of us humanities consultants. I expect he had hoped we wouldn't be so pasty and smiley as we were.

Third example of being unconscious of enemies: propagating oak trees

Of all instances of creatures' having enemies this is the simplest: the enemies of small oak trees. I am telling this anecdote last because I got it through my head last—two years ago—consciously, and because propagating any plants, laying out the simplest garden, involves us in battling the enemies of those plants. Yet one meets gardeners who don't notice that concept. They may weed the garden, but what they talk is *nurture*.

---

[4] Hamlin Garland's memoir is called *A Son of the Middle Border.* His best stories are collected in *Main Travelled Roads.*

For ten years I have been growing oak trees from acorns, with the idea of returning 7 acres of northern Minnesota pasture to forest. I have instinctively cleared quack grass and hawk's eye weed from the baby trees, and set about killing the ever springing-up willow bushes. It took me years to realize that stopping the depredations on the baby oaks was the most important task of raising the trees. Being a woman I had heard how nourishing we women are and that nourishing equals helping others. Protecting from predators hadn't a tenth of the cachet that fertilizing plants had.

Oak trees will be the handsome long-term survivors of low-level global heating. The firs of Minnesota are already retreating northward at the average rate of a half-mile a year, reseeding themselves on their northern sides. But oak trees can bear heat better, and hold their crowns over the soil to keep it cooler. Growing oaks, therefore, had a hold on me. Human nature is averse to realizing enemies, however. It took me years to realize that the oaks would go about collecting their own nourishment. What the baby trees needed in me was a giant ally to keep their enemies at bay. I was needed to keep willows from sending roots through their roots, and the hawk's eye weed from setting out poison so that they couldn't thrive in their places, and the quack from wrapping its eerie white tendrils around the oaks' central root to strangle it.

I needed to have used my imagination about their needs long before I did. The human mental balking against acknowledging the presence of serious enemies is absolutely amazing. We know that the English, with the exception of Churchill, who in the 1930s hired his own spies to keep in touch with what the Nazis were hatching up, resisted realizing that Nazi Germany was shaping up as the most serious enemy of their empire. We know that Jews in Hungarian villages resisted the very idea that Nazis were incarcerating, torturing, gassing to death, then incinerating Jews even when an escaping Jew dragged himself back especially to warn them. Elie Wiesel tells his terrible story of how the Jews of Sighet, his village, jeered to Moche the Beadle when he tried to warn them. Even when the Germans showed up to occupy their town, people denied the need to worry.

"The [German] officers were billeted in private houses, even in the homes of Jews. Their attitude toward
their hosts was distant, but polite. They never demand-
ed the impossible, made no unpleasant comments, and
even smiled occasionally at the mistress of the house.
One German officer lived in the house opposite ours.
He had a room with the Kahn family. They said he was
a charming man—calm, likable, polite, and sympathetic.
Three days after he moved in he brought Madame
Kahn a box of chocolates. The optimists rejoiced.

'Well, there you are, you see! What did we tell
you? You wouldn't believe us. There they are *your*
Germans! What do you think of them? Where is their
famous cruelty?'"⁵

The most important enemies that privileged Americans have in
2004 are very likely psychological enemies. That is, they are the
friends, mentors, teachers, and other acquaintance who consciously or unconsciously want the educated, therefore lucky, American
not to fulfill his or her capacity for empathic, moral imagination.

Sometimes those teachers and friends can see how *imagining
others*, even when the others are suffering, changes the person
doing the imagining. Those looking on feel left out of it. They
gently say things: you are being too hard on yourself, or you
have a right to be laid back. If you are not laid back it makes
them cross as bears.

I was facilitating a class at Emerson School in Duluth. The ele-
mentary-school teacher whose class I joined for one day of my
five at the school refused to stay in the room while I helped the
children develop a story. She announced her refusal in a rude
tone.

The children and I worked up a story about the town dump.
Gunny sacks full of kittens got left off there by cruel human
adults, and children escaped dangerous houses by going to live at
the dump. Other animals, having already taken up residence in
the dump, knew their way around. They helped the children find

⁵ Elie Wiesel, *The Night Trilogy*, Hill and Wang, New York, 1972, page 19

sauce pans to cook with and food that had not yet rotted. The dump was clearly a dream. Gradually more and more children, the shyer ones now, raised their hands to add some detail that they visualized. I asked each child a question about what he or she had just said, so they each got a chance not just to shout an inspiration, but to refine it a little. I thanked each for contributing but sometimes did not enlarge on the details with the class. One child said that a child entered the dump who had been beaten so hard by "someone back home" that the child escaped to the dump.

Soon there were only a few kids who had not yet contributed. I thought some of them looked a little lethargic. Perhaps they were mainstreamed kids of less ability than the general run. I told the class we needed animal sounds—the meowing of cats and barking of dogs and growling of pigs. Pigs don't growl, someone pointed out. "Ah you're right about that. No growling of pigs," I said. One of the children who hadn't spoken yet said "Bears growl." "Will you be the bear, so that each time we need the bear to growl I'll give you the high sign and you growl?"

It all went very well, but once just in the middle, the elementary teacher emerged from the little rear office where she was correcting papers. She tried to dart out of the rear door without my stopping her. No good. "Come join us," I shouted to her. "We'll catch you up on the story so far!"

"No way!" she snapped back.

I thought, well, you can go to hell, too. We were natural enemies, she and I, but there was something more important about this. What if no one all her life had ever asked her to imagine a dump full of the creatures who have been deprived of justice but now have formed a slightly incredible, heartening alliance among themselves? What if not just her school teachers, when she was young, but everyone she knew had jeered or scolded when her drawings didn't stay within the lies? What if no one like William Wordsworth or Antonio Damasio or Gerald Edelman had ever told her, "Stay *outside* the lines! Come out of there, trust your own lines!"

Her enemy, our kill-joy culture, had got inside her and convinced her not to play with the re-entrant faculties of her brain.

At some level, however, her brain knew it could *have enjoyed reentrant thinking*, so now she felt galled.

This book is mainly for educated people who so far haven't felt much pain over American neo-conservatism, but now are every day less easy in their minds. How shall we apply the discussions above? How shall we identify who is the enemy of such and such a creature? We should deliberately, like those people who read a lot of Virginia Woolf in the 1950s and could hardly believe that she was writing for *them*—deliberately make lists of *our* enemies.

If we have secure income and inside us somewhere the kind of college education that makes a person able to translate sense impressions into abstract concepts if need be, let's consider those enemies of our lives that we could call *psychological enemies*. The most frightening of all. But we can get around them.

The best gift of psychology to normal people is truth where previously we've lived with lies. It sounds odd to say it, but lies more than other social abuse jerk their victims around. An example: the kind of folk wisdom that runs rampant among upper-class folk blames the victim. Proper psychology frees the victim. If the victim is a peaceable person, he or she may never go after whoever the perpetrator was who had spoiled life until then. If the victim is an activist, he or she might decide to change, as they say, the world.

A major interruption here: if there is one quality in liberals that drives anyone who must do business nuts or anyone who writes books nuts it is this one exclamation that liberals keep making: "I just can't understand how so and so (some conservative leader or follower) can *say* (or *do*) things like that!"

Their exclamation responds to the wrong question. Our interest should be not in how someone got to be the way they are but in how it is that they have not yet turned out some other way. Say we think back to Chapter 5 in which Wordsworth is talking about how he works on impressions and ideas within his own mind, and the neuroscientist Gerald Edelman says that the brain "is more in touch with itself than with anything else." Those are amazing statements. They are the more amazing if you ask yourself, "If it is a potential for members of homo sapiens to weigh each new impression against all our older feelings and conclusions so far, why do we do it so seldom? Here is a list of rea-sons—psychological enemies that operate to despoil our better imaginations.

Psychological enemies of the privileged heretofore conservative

Family solidarity

Families almost uniformly describe themselves as an organiza-tion that enhances the life of each family member. Paul C. Rosenblatt's *Metaphors of Family Systems Theory* [6] gives a fascinat-ing account of how the very phrasing of conversations in families can keep lies going. A family can be unconsciously or at least unconfessedly organized to benefit not the whole group but very particularly the father or the mother. Children get sacrificed to their parents' goals. American, British, and German literatures are a rich treasury of intense fiction about imperialism practiced in families without anyone's noticing it.[7]

Brenda Ueland wrote a perfect essay showing how a child's own moral growth can be waylaid or stalled by insidious, compla-cent family-solidarity.[8] Ueland asked a class what they liked to do best. Sally explained that she loved herding deer. Her father took her up into the north woods. She disappeared into the thicket and chased the wild deer out toward him. Then he killed it with bow and arrow. Ueland allowed it sounded hard on the deer. Sally said that sometimes "the poor deer drags for miles and miles and there is blood over everything." She loves her father. She now, since a good teacher made her describe it in her own voice, found that she suffered. She did not completely "love" herding deer, then. The teacher was not trained in professional empathy, so she couldn't help Sally get to the place where she could divide attachment to the father from her own sense of mercy. As it was, for the sake of natural family love, Sally had kept her own sense of mercy unconscious.

---

[6] New York: The Guilford Press, 72 Spring St., New York, NY 10012, 1994.
[7] Edith Wharton's *The Age of Innocence*, Anthony Trollope's *The Pallisers*, and Thomas Mann's *Buddenbrooks* come to mind.
[8] Brenda Ueland, "Herding Deer," in *Strength to your Sword Arm: Selected Writings*. Duluth: Holy Cow! Press, 1992, pp 175-178.

The crude morality of corporate workplaces

In the appendix of this book we have a generous group of passages by the psychologist Douglas LaBier. He studied upper-level corporate workplace misery and how it horribly subjects one's kinder feelings to one's merely practical, group-persuaded feeling. Because LaBier's observations are so intricate and professional we asked and gratefully received permission to put much original source in our appendix. Please do see his remarks. No one could write with more feeling about how careerism in this last past century takes a toll on promising executives. The workplace morality, or immorality, seemed to be inimical to the best in homo sapiens.

Fear of losing sexual panache

The ancient street expression, "All's fair in love and war" roughly blankets an interesting dilemma for modern unemployed spouses of well-to-do conservatives. They need to be, and we will use the word that is now so politically incorrect but which still means what it has always meant and still calls up the relevant delights or terrors, "attractive." A rich man's spouse has to be attractive.

The difficulty is that being attractive has to maintain at least a modicum of strong secularity. The Chinese used to say that thought itself spoiled the perfect vacuum that men want in a woman's face—a wildly retro sexist remark. Still, sexual attraction has to do with brain centers other than reciprocal upper-cortex messaging. A drop of ascetic holiness can instantly spoil the lot. This works in both males and females, likely because earnestness, a wonderful quality in talking about some aspect, let's say, of one's unified philosophy makes someone listening respond from very different neuronal centers from those in which desire lights up.

Apart from sexual desire as being secular, there is another especially secular aspect of sexual attraction. It is *tricksterism*. Someone who has the panache to "work the system," so to speak, is likely to be more sexually attractive that a non-jocular pilgrim of any sort. Of the March sisters in *Little Women*, the one with sexual éclat was always Amy, who took the world as it was and devoted herself to charming everybody and preserving the class system.

Another ethics-neutral aspect of sexual charm is fragmented conversation. On the East coast of the United States it is considered attractive for a woman to be able to maintain a kind of filmy, flexing, fragmented conversation. It is less attractive to be speaking from a unified philosophy. By the very rich, I have been told verbatim not once but twice that a woman's conversation should be a tennis game played from the baseline. Send a ball. It comes back into your court. Send some other shot. It comes back. It is all a game, and games are more attractive than any sticky opinion. Besides, a good many business executives, males or females, know that conversation in living rooms is conversation in living rooms. It should be in charming fragments.

That puts some pressure on anyone wishing to go deeper. This isn't necessarily a reason to go on voting Republican though, since how one votes is a constitutional secret. But it might split a person's consciousness a little. Jim Harrison's very great story, originally in *The New Yorker* and later collected with two others, "The Woman Lit by Fireflies," takes a long look at the rich, unemployed wife's psychology. Harrison is the only author who seems to have actually understood how she would be thwarted from developing her own ethical take on things.

The expectation of being in groups most of the time

So many people have clamored and wept on the subject of lack of solitude in our time, and how the lack will worsen in future time, we won't discuss it more. Being in the constant presence of others blocks people' growth.

A list of sentences to protect a human being who is in the throes of becoming deeper.

We would like to present a list of sentences that readers can memorize to have ready in case an enemy to your imagination should offer to give you a cuff or two. A trick to not being blind-sided is to have a small repertoire of responses to make if suddenly accosted. If we get far enough so we can acknowledge that some people will oppose us every time we try to be "good," as Louisa May Alcott used to say only half ironically, because she was half in earnest, then we know we need an invisible shield or two.

Shields have to be specialized for the individual job. That is, graphite soaks up the playout of Uranium 235, present-day body armour stops bullets. The sentences below are specifically for protecting anxious, conscientious people who find themselves being obliquely confronted or outright insulted by people they love. The sentences keep the relationship going but save you eating crow or being word-whipped or bullied in any way.

A word for those who ought to rethink whatever confidence they have in just plain good manners: helping professionals, whom you may automatically not respect so much as you respect the living room courtesies learnt from your parents and their courteous friends, have identified four kinds of really *non-communication* that pass for good manners when someone has brought up some public issue. Even the United States Department of State teaches the spouses of its foreign service personnel two of these four dysfunctional styles because, from the point of view of the State Department, families of State Department people are only adjuncts. They need have no valuable opinions of their own, so their job, at any of the receptions that personnel and their spouses have to attend when serving abroad, is solely to keep push from becoming shove. When people are standing around balancing half-glasses of drinks but wisely not drinking much, the best, most traditional way to head off trouble is to keep the conversation animated (you must look interested) but extraordinarily boring. "How are the children?" you can ask. Small talk is death to people who want to think and who believe in human beings enough to think that others might like to think, too. We mention this as a reminder that all purposes in a living room are not the same. A style dysfunctional for serious thinkers might be just the thing for spouses of foreign service personnel.

The four dysfunctional styles of communication, then:

1. Jeering: you say some serious thing that infuriates them. They jeer at you: "Well, isn't that just typical of a bleeding-heart liberal?" …"so out of touch with the real world!"

2. *Ad hominem* insult: You announce some theory they don't like the sound of: they make a personal attack on you. This is called making *ad hominem* (to the person) remarks. Example: you say you are ashamed of America for attacking Iraq. They return: "Yes, but you have never been a really loyal citizen. You are not the kind of person who will stand by our troops."

3. Distraction: You say you are afraid that American civil liberties might further disappear. They say, with a glance at your cup or plate or glass: "You know what? You need a refill! Let me fix that!"

4. Trivialization by focusing on a fraction of something said. You say you are frightened by the increasing difference in income between the few wealthy and the masses of poor. They say, and to carry this off they have to speak as animatedly as they can: "A propos, the internet is more and more amazing in how you can get people's statistics, even their income statistics if you get onto the right data bases. Sometimes I just can't believe how much robust information is out there!"

Those are the four bad styles. Here are some quick replies that help you not bite any bullets that you shouldn't be biting. They preserve your privacy, but they allow for love and friendship to continue between speakers if love and friendship do exist between the speakers in question.

Civilized sentences especially for people waking to their inner philosophies

Sentences to stand off intrusive questions you should not deal with at all.

Someone says, "So how *are* you going to vote, anyway?

A sentence to try: Actually, nothing exciting. Just constitutionally, by secret ballot.
Someone says, "Poverty is a state of mind."[9]
A sentence to try: I know. Poverty is like being hanged. Being hanged is a state of mind unless you're Nathan Hale, of course.

A sentence that lets you stand up for your point of view that occasionally serves, what's more, to keep the discussion rational and civilized.

Someone says: "I think this whole thing is making a very big mountain out of a very small molehill."
A sentence to try: Actually, I am on the other side.[10] [Authors' note: this is the best sentence of them all. It is surprising and confrontative and courteous.]

A sentence to head off rhetorical prophesying

Someone says: "You know what'll happen if the Congress does such and such? The whole country will etc., etc."
A sentence to try: We don't know that, actually.

Sentences to handle irritability over political issues that come up typically between spouses, partners, or lovers

Someone says: "Sounds to me as if you are abandoning everything the family stands for. Frankly, that's what it sounds like to me."
A sentence to try: It may sound like that, but I am not doing it.
Someone says: "You used to have a good sense of humor. You probably still have one, but I'm certainly not seeing much of it these days."
A sentence to try: You're right. [Never argue with anyone who says you have lost or are losing your sense of humor.]

---

[9] Replying to a question by a member of the House Financial Services Committee, on May 20, 2004, Secretary Alphonso Jackson of the U.S. Department of Housing and Urban Development (HUD) stated that "being poor is a state of mind, not a condition".
[10] If use of the word "actually" annoys you, don't use it. We like it because it slows the sentence, it has a modest tone, it cuts any abruptness that might seem rude.

Someone says: "Well, one thing I've learned in this world is you need a sense of humor. Couldn't you lighten up some?"
A sentence to try: Actually, probably not. I apologize though.[11]

Sentences for when your new way of withdrawing from the living room into your own thinking has already made friends uneasy and angry.

You have not said, "I now keep my counsel," but people feel it. Cautiously, they start around the edges of this (for them) problem...They are poised to express anger but inside themselves to feel fear. They want to be nice persons, though, so instead of saying "You used to be nice but now you're not" they put on a wise expression and imply that you must be under some unfortunate psychological pressure. If they are really shameless they add, "I hope everything's OK with you and Megan."

Someone says: "You seem to be changing your mind a lot".
A sentence to try: I think you're right. I feel as if I am.

Someone says: "Somehow I don't feel as if I really know you any more."
A sentence to try: I'm still here, but I'm thinking.

Someone says: "Well, frankly, all this is over *my* head."
A sentence to try: Or not. It may be over your head, but I doubt it. Maybe it is over *mine* too. Still, I'm interested.

Some rebuttals look all right on the page but all they are is rebuttals. For example, if someone says, "Cool it! I was just kidding!" it's no good making a sarcastic remark like "I know. Virginia Woolf and Thomas Paine were just kidding, too." Sarcasm only says my philosophy is more profound than yours, a spoken or unspoken comment that people pick up on like lightning. It

---

[11] Something to teach children: to say "I apologize" instead of "I'm sorry" since they may not be sorry, in which case we have asked them to lie. And you may not be sorry that you can't lighten up, too. There is no literal value to saying "I apologize" when someone says you lack humor and you aren't so much fun as you used to be, etc., but it has a stubborn ring to it. When overly critical people hear that stubborn ring, they back up.

used to surprise me that people who constantly advise others to
"lighten up" actually don't want to be told that they themselves
have succeeded in lightening up and now are light-weights. Here
is why: at some level, perhaps because we have been taught passionate ideas of famous people like George Washington and
Abraham Lincoln and Socrates and Wang Dan[12] we know, even if
only half-consciously, that profound-and-passionate are better
than shallow-and-kidding. The idea is in there that we could be
doing profound and passionate if we'd only get up for it.
Therefore, people verbally committed to a "fun life" are always
unsteady inside themselves somewhere.

We make an image of our ourselves as a fun person. Let's
now pretend that someone lays some photographs across our
knees. Several photographs. Private First Class Lynndie England
and Specialist Sabrina Harman and Megan Ambuhl. A second picture shows three fellows in the Germans' Special Police Battalion
101 doing World War II service in Poland. They are young men,
one smiling at the camera as he stands with one foot on the chest
of a just killed Jew. The others around him are smiling, too. They
are not sadists. They are smiling for the picture because having
your picture taken can be fun.

I continue imagining myself a fun person. I will look up at
whoever wished those pictures on me, some holier-than-thou
family member, and say, "Listen, I don't have to deal with this.
You mind your business. I'll mind mine."

Perhaps the fun person will drift along imperfectly but work-
ably happy. It is always amazing how long people can manage
not to think much of anything, not to feel much of anything, not
to decide to do any ethical project even if they got the idea two
decades ago. A perfect case is General George Lee Butler. General
Butler announced in Washington on December 4th, 1996, that the

[12] Arrested after the Tiananmen Square massacre in 1989, Wang Dan was held in prison for 6
years, most of it in solitary confinement. While in prison he went through his thoughts wonder-
ing how the bloodshed might have been avoided. Later, however, Wang wrote that "Indeed,
one of the real tragedies of 1989 was not that we jeopardized the efforts of so-called reformist
leaders but that Communist leaders, be they conservatives or reformist, are all wedded to retain-
ing the current political system...—From *The Scotsman*, June 3, 2004. Also in *The Wall Street
Journal.*
[13] Colman McCarthy, "General's Conversion a Non-Bombshell," *The Washington Post*, December
17, 1996, page D23.

United States nuclear policy was "fundamentally irrational."[13] While in the Air Force General Butler had approved thousands of sites to be annihilated with nuclear weaponry. He earned four stars. Then, well into an apparently unashamed retirement, making no confessions, making no apologies, he announced that he was enjoying "the luxury to step back mentally and think about the implications of having spent 4 trillion dollars and producing 70,000 nuclear weapons." Nothing he said, according to the report, however, suggested that he felt that his prominent role in nuclear weaponry had anything nefarious about it.

It is an example of delay in "stepping back," to use the General's phrase for *thinking with some perspective*, in addition to feeling no guilt. If we imagine ourselves married to someone more principled than we are—someone who has just asked us to *feel* something that we don't yet feel—say, sorrow or compunction— while looking at photographs of murderous human behavior in the name of patriotic war making, we may snarl "I don't have to deal with this! You mind your business and I'll mind mine!"

A lot of fun people manage to stay fun people all their lives. Position and income and the lucky fact of American citizenship allow it. And everybody who is raised by caring adults is a fun person until the moment when they are made *afraid* by something.

A fun person may be straggling along the neuronal paths across the cortex. He or she may be starting to suffer in the way that feeling responsible for one's government makes people suffer. It is hard to tell from the outside whether or not the fun person has started to let himself or herself feel compassionate to people who will always be strangers far away, speaking some other language.

We ought to figure that the fun person may be just starting to learn about the loneliness of moral people who live in fun settings. There are all sorts of psychological settings that are more lonely, such as Wang Dan's years in solitary, but still, starting to take life seriously while living in a confident, complacent setting is lonely work. One's own living room can be lonely, if one's living room is full of confident, complacent people whom you love.

The person just leaving the fun outlook might feel afraid, yet willing and wanting, actually, to think about fearful things.

Ideally there should be some sentences that person could say aloud or sentences that people who have been there could say to him or her. They would want to welcome the fun person to a very scary, still hopeful kind of American citizenship.

A Very
Small Bibliography to Introduce People
To some Up-to-date Neurological Thinking

Damasio, Antonio R., *Descartes' Error: Emotion, Reason, and the Human Brain*. New York: G.P.Putnam's Sons (A Grosset/Putnam Book), 1994.

Damasio, Antonio R., *The Feeling of What Happens: Body and Emotion in the Making of Consciousness*. San Diego: Harcourt,Inc. (A Harvest Book), 1999.

Damasio, Antonio R., *Looking for Spinoza: Joy, Sorrow, and the Feeling Brain*. New York: Harcourt, Inc., 2003.

Edelman, Gerald M., *The Remembered Present: A Biological Theory of Consciousness*. New York: Basic Books, 1989.

Edelman, Gerald M., *Bright Air, Brilliant Fire: On the Matter of the Mind*. New York: BasicBooks, 1992.

Edelman, Gerald M., *Wider Than the Sky: the Phenomenal Gift of Consciousness*. New Haven: Yale University Press, 2004

Edelman, Gerald M., and Tononi, Giulio, *A Universe of Consciousness: How Matter Becomes Imagination*. New York: BasicBooks, 1992.

LaBier, Douglas, Modern Madness: *The Hidden Link Between Work and Emotional Conflict*. New York: Simon & Schuster Inc, A Touchstone Book,1986

Ledoux, Joseph, *The Emotional Brain: The Mysterious Underpinnings of Emotional Life*. New York: Simon & Schuster, 1996. LeDoux is referred to in Damasio, *Looking for Spinoza,* too.

Ledoux, Joseph, *Synaptic Self: How Our Brains Become Who We Are*. New York: Viking-Penguin, 2002.

Panksepp, Jaak "Feeling the Pain of Social Loss" *Science*, Vol.302 10 October, 2003, www.sciencemag.org
The author is at the J.P. Scott Center for Neuroscience, Mind Behavior, Dept of Psychology, Bowling Green State University, Bowling Green, OH 43403, and at the Falk Center for Molecular Therapeutics, Dept of Biomedical Engineering, Northwestern University, Evanston, IL 60201,

Panksepp, Jaak. *Affective Neuroscience: The Foundations of Human and Animal Emotions*. New York: Oxford University Press, 1998. Cited in Antonio Damasio, *Looking for Spinoza* on p.303 notes and p.307 notes.

Ridley, Matt, *Genome: The Autobiography of a Species in 23 Chapters*, HarperCollins, 1999.

Sapolsky, Robert, *Biology and Human Behavior. The Neurological Origins of Individuality*. Chantilly, VA 20151-1232: The Teaching Company (An audio book, Course No. 179 in the Great Courses Series).

Wordsworth, William, "Preface to Lyrical Ballads, Second Edition," 1800. This poet made the cut in our neuroscience bibliography because of his scrupulous discussion of the difference between his feelings about the ideas made from previous sense impressions and the feelings about the original sense impressions—a neat century and a half before most people knew enough to rejoice in that distinction. The "Preface.."
nearly presages Gerald Edelman's comment, when writing about re-entry, that "the brain is more in touch with itself than with anything else." See also Wordsworth's famous and variously understood and misunderstood poem, "Ode: Intimations of Immortality from Recollections of Early Childhood".

A Handsome Reading List

"The Woman Lit by Fireflies" by Jim Harrison
   A woman elegantly brought up to jeer at her own earliest compassion by socially high-end parents struggles to free herself of a blackguard of a management husband—but not in time to have stood up against him for her own daughter. Jim Harrison has the literary franchise in rich women. Unlike most novels, this one contains no wild guesses. Harrison *knows*.

The Liberty Campaign by Jonathan Dee
   The world is full of businessman-gets-moral novels, but this one is remarkable in that although the protagonist becomes aware of the fallout of bad work on those who can't help themselves, he still betrays everything in sight, even the dog of the victim before he is done.

Little Women by Louisa May Alcott
   A book naturally read for the terrific story of 4 American girls' growing up. For a possible rereading, note the difference between the 4 girls' adaptation to the classical moral issues of uneven playing fields for the poor, the uneven playing field of women, and whether or not one should be a change agent or not. Other major moral issues, such as war, never come into this most self-consciously moral of all moral novels. Alcott was a genius at seeing the difference between change agents and go-alongs.

   Meg , as a creature of the system
   Jo, as a class-system change agent
   Beth, genius at household and community love and the ability to sacrifice herself for others more than all her sisters put together.
   Amy: a 100% self-oriented and confident worker-of-the-system. Was going to marry for money or title. Does even better. Married Laurie and becomes a conservative "Lady Bountiful" of noblesse oblige.

"Neighbour Rosicky" by Willa Cather.

This is one of the 10 greatest American short stories ever written, for a number of reasons which readers and critics have appreciated. An unusual way to look at this story is as the story of a man who chose to do the original thing in about every case, not the thing a man of his background or farm community would naturally glide into.

"Gooseberries" by Anton Chekhov.

A story about how a niche-idea (such as wanting a gooseberry farm) can like any addiction make its human victim wreck his chances to have a genuine philosophy of life, and work cruelly against those around him.

War and Peace by Leo Tolstoy.

For readers who tend to reread War and Peace now and again in life, we suggest thinking of it as a strange, rambling discussion of how slow people are to grow up to generativity. All of the characters, especially Pierre Bezhukov, the protagonist, mine their privileges for ages before deciding whether they shouldn't actually stand up for some notion of what life's about. Even then, Pierre was horribly slow in getting to see that what was really happening was dreadful and that he must drop his blithe Boy Scoutisms.

Getting Brave Enough to Become Conscious and to Stay Conscious of Uncomfortable Truths and to Take Counsel with Oneself: A Stage Development Philosophy

We offer this strand of moral-stage-development theory with gratitude to Jane Loevinger for the inspiration of her work, Ego Development, and in grateful memory of the imaginative thinking of Lawrence Kohlberg[1]

A note to those not used to stage-development philosophy. The abiding idea of it is that people go through all the stages in order, until they get to the stage at which they get stuck. Those not abused and those educated in talking over ideas with others when young tend to get through the early stages faster than those in homes where conversation is scarce and only about concrete practicalities. Still, the brain is programmed with the *potential* for everyone to refine feeling and thinking as we use our brains to look at the world. The strange but replicable documentation is that as the brain functions, it changes, and it becomes ever more able to think novel thoughts, and disagreeable truths, and to feel sympathy for others. No one skips a stage. The stages are not age related because they depend so very much on the psychological circumstances of the individual person's life. (For example, children bullied by parents are slower to leave stage 4 authority-accepting and get to thinking for themselves than children whose spirits haven't been stalled by fear or by insult.) Some people get stuck in stage one. Very likely most modern human beings get stuck in stages 3 and 4—letting their ideas be influenced by peers

[1] Dr Loevinger, professor *emerita* of Washington University, St Louis, did much of her work at the University of Minnesota as well as at Washington University. Lawrence Kohlberg is known as the father of modern moral stage-development philosophy. He did most of his work at Harvard. After his death his papers were brought from Larsen Hall at Harvard to the University of Minnesota. His work has been demonized by an early gender-specific enclave of the women's movement. There are stage-development philosophers previous to and contemporary to Kohlberg and Loevinger—but these two are accessible, original, and generous-minded. Earlier interesting stage-development thinkers include, oddly enough, Friedrich Schiller and later, George Orwell, well before the famous Erik Erikson and Henry Sullivan.

and by those in authority over them. Millions of people, however, get to stage 5, when they can think for themselves and even design their own behavior to agree with their own philosophies. Stage 6 is a logical step after stage 5, but very likely billions of human beings never reach stage 6. It takes a lot of imagination actually to notice what life is for those far away whom we will never meet, and for non-human creatures of our planet whom we will never see, or for plants. It takes still more courageous imagination to have compassion for those far away in *time*—those still unborn.

1. Conscious of one's own discomforts, not that of others.
   This stage is an *amoral*, selfish stage. You can't get a nursing baby to understand that it should relinquish the breast for a quarter hour because a third-world child is starving and needs it more. They won't get it. Babies are quintessential stage 1 people, and it suits their age group. When people get *stuck* at stage 1 as adults we call them sociopaths.

2. Conscious of good or ill happening to one's own tribe or family only.
   This second level of awareness is still so self-serving that most stage-development moralists regard it as a "pre-moral" level of thinking. It is very we/they oriented. Our family, our tribe, our church are good, our nation, too, if we imagine that far out from home (a lot of people don't). We feel pain if our family or tribe or church or nation suffers somehow, but as for the others, they are just landscape, or colonial territories to be mined, or vague shadows in our minds. In terms of behavior (as opposed to growth of awareness), most foreign policies are run by Stage 2 philosophy: our interests are what count, not theirs. When one hires a defense attorney one contracts for him or her to be *a creature of our interests*, not anyone else's.
   An interesting aspect of this very tribal stage: it is *pre*-philosophical by definition, just in the fact that we in stage 2 consider *our* well-being, not someone else's. A stage 2 person can use any means to further the tribal well-being.
   Tricksterism is natural to this tribal stage of development. Most of the folk tales collected in the 18th and 19th centuries in

Germany by the Grimm Brothers, in Norway by Asbjørnsen and Moe, in Denmark by Bp. Nikolai F.S. Grundtvig, and the Japanese fairy tales brought into English by Yei Theodora Ozaki in 1904, are stories of practical trickery. The tribal heroes stand up to the evil cunning of non-tribal villains. Someone insults, assaults or kills one of our fellows: we typically get help from some tricky warrior or counselor of our own. We bring to bear some satisfying, generally horrible punishment upon the evil doer. To tricksters any methods that *work* are good. Agreeable stuff, but still, it is a relief, after reading folk literature, to take up a *literary* story teller like Hans Christian Andersen. Folk literature tends towards either kidding about village fools and trolls or about practical ways to repulse assault by the neighbors or extended-family members. Literature tends to be about wisdom versus provincial prejudice and about universal tragic qualities of human life vs reciprocal violent behaviors. Examples: "The Ugly Duckling" is about how anyone more refined than the common denominator will be treated cruelly by provincials. "The Little Match Girl" is about the constant presence of poverty. Andersen's "Great Claus and Little Claus" is about a skillful trickster who outwits and deceives.

Tricky people typically work the system very well. For one thing, they have no conscientious dislike of the system, so they are comfortable with it. In *Little Women* Amy studied the system very carefully and played it with great skill. She was an utterly practical person for whom idealism was a passing whiff of Roman Catholic piety when a young girl. Her true love was the Real World, shown in the conversation with Jo after one of their disastrous "calls" made on an afternoon. When I first read Scott Russell Sanders's beautiful lines about tricky minds I thought of Amy.

"...We speak of God's thoughts as if we could read them; but we read only by the dim light of a tricky brain on a young planet near a middling star."[2]

I revere Sanders's pointing out that our brains are tricky because in our early years and in comparatively primitive folk cul-

---

[2] Scott Russell Sanders, in *The Georgia Review*, Spring, 1997, page 126.

tures trickiness is what we do. Once modern human beings are forty, if they are still tricksters, there is nothing about any stage-development philosophy that wouldn't make them grin and roll their eyes. There are a number of reasons why liberals repeatedly are shocked by the scorn of tricky operators for anything like conscience. Liberals should check out the possibility that many a flagrant doer of bad works is a Stage 2 person for whom the trickier the means to the further well-being of one's tribe or country the more gratifying the project. After all, we want our spies to be liars and tricksters. We don't want our case litigated by a stage 6 person who might decide that in the broad scheme of things, we, the client, should serve some time.

Most mammals and millions of *homines sapientes* are guided by Stage 2 thinking: "Sorry, but we give to our church" and "Look, we've got our kids to think of, you know." A person in stage 2 tribalism would feel very uneasy if advised to feel and think on behalf of someone outside his or her own tribe. These are the people Goering referred to in his famous assurance to Hitler that he could count on dissenting people's neighbors to turn them in for treason if they aren't enthusiastic about whatever war Hitler wants to start. Whenever a government starts a war, there are a good many non-intellectuals who decide that their local intellectual is a traitor. Kohlberg pointed out that people especially resent those in moral-feeling states just above their own: thus a tribal stage 2 person might easily resent intellectuals' constant talking as if they were stage 5 people (whether they were or not), so a declaration of war gives the tribal person a chance to gouge back.

3. Taking our Style from our Peers.
Peer group guiding. In this stage whatever one's peer group is doing is right. This is a perfectly understandable stage for pre-teen and teen people to be in. They need to get free of their parents' ideas. They don't want to dress the way their parents think they should. They want to be like the kids of the "good" crowd. Probably most human beings stay in stage 3 or stage 4 all their lives. C.S. Lewis's sharp-edged essay, "The Inner Ring," is about peer-group social climbing. Stage 3 works. No one in any culture

gets imprisoned or hanged for imitating the neighbors. And guiding by peers has some good points: say your family is made up of thugs and slobs and generally negligent human beings or outright crooks. If you have some peers to set your style by in school you might get out of the family hole.

Some people stay in Stage 3 all their lives. This suits them for certain endeavors. This can be a lifelong stage especially for groupies. Groupies are capable of idealism. They will feel the need when the group is stressed and sometimes bravely serve those needs. They seek peer approval, of course, which means they serve the group in ways that groups tend to approve of. They do not tend to help the group learn anything about psychology, but they are willing to suit up in the uniform of their country and risk their lives for it, because groups, especially of people aged 14 to 21, believe in armed service.

Groupiness isn't admirable even as mere socialization, however. It prohibits the growth of feeling. Group members sink to the common denominator as fast as rocks fall through clear water to the mud bottom, because if a group is going to stay happy its members must suppress admiration for excellence of any kind. The whole group can't be excellent. They know that. To them it is just poor public relations to distinguish the excellent workers from the rest, so their ideal is *good relations*, not admiration of the beautiful or true or any other high-minded universal. If one spends one's babyhood in daycare, one's early childhood in daycare or on the streets, and the rest of one's school-day life in large classrooms, one is always in groups. Millions thus experience very few hours with one mentor (as in Mom or Dad) or a teacher with a small enough class so he or she can actually talk ideas with the kids.

Here is an interesting particular anecdote showing how groupiness can work against people even *recognizing excellence*. In a scrupulously careful yet much-encompassing review of a book called *Contemporary Poetry*, Judith Kitchen acknowledges that the anthology covers a useful broad swath of poets born after 1910. She names several schools of poetry well-represented—the New York school, the Beat Generation, the Black Mountain school, and others. She writes: "These additions are welcome; they will deepen classroom discussion and offer a variety of models for aspiring writers." And then she gets to her complaint over the lack of attention to excellence: "But I quarrel with some of the proportions. So much Snodgrass and so little Stafford? Or so much Clampitt, so little Stafford? So much Baraka, so little Stafford? So much Bidart, so little Stafford? Not that it takes more space to make more impact, but that space here is one scale of 'worth.'"[3]

The intensity of universal feeling in William Stafford's work, his gift for passionate ideas, his marvelous images that we love for they seem like everyday experience that we know about, but with a deeper take on that day than we likely gave it—all of that huge gift of an excellent poet shouldn't be only a pleasant small presence along with a capable group of practioners work. Love of excellence gets trampled faster by stage 3 groupies than by any other means besides the exorbitant cultural destruction that takes place when people stop teaching the young to read. That is the cause of Judith Kitchen's rightful indignation.

Note: Stages 3 and 4 overlap a good deal. Those who take their beliefs from their peer group typically take their moral counsel from authority figures or organizations in their lives. In the army, for example, one must at least seem to be loyal to the authority figures (drill instructors, officers, the President of the United States as commander-in-chief). One's peer group is at the largest, one's outfit, or company; most usually recruits and soldiers have most feeling for their own squads and platoons. In religious life, in the most authoritarian religions (Islam, fundamentalist Christianity, to give two examples) one's sympathies are nearly always with other members of one's congregation or faith.

4. The stage at which one reveres authority and is hardly brave enough to think any thought or feel any feeling without having received orders.

Stage 4 is what makes servants good servants, enlisted men good soldiers, battered women faithful wives, chicken-minded people good fascists, and so on. You don't respect your own con-

[3] Judith Kitchen, "Anthologizing—the Good, the Bad, and the Indifferent," *The Georgia Review*, Winter, 2003, on page 861

science in this stage: you do what the boss says, period. The book and the movie, *Remains of the Day*, is about Stage 4 behavior in two connected settings—Nazism in Germany and ethical stunting in the British servant class. A brilliant piece of moral literature. It's very hard to graduate from Stage 4, the authority obeying stage, to Stage 5, by the way, because in Stage 4 you're all the time near or with buddies and your leader of one sort or another is hovering near in a comforting way. You feel safe. You feel valuable as a citizen. If you went to stage 5, you would find yourself standing alone.

"Political Conservatism as motivated Social Cognition" is a fascinating psychological study of what looks basically like a stage 4 mentality.[4] This very professional paper is full of interpretations we can try for fit on authority-admiring people. One of the liveliest statements is Professor's Glaser's comment that "liberals appear to have a higher tolerance for change than conservatives do." In a section called "Evidence Linking Epistemic, Existential, and Ideological Motives to Political Conservatism," the authors discuss their findings on how conservatism relates to several mindsets. We need to bear in mind that people pass *through* stages. People now exemplifying stage 4 admiration of authority may graduate to the more courageous stage 5, of thinking one's own thoughts, and reading one's own newspapers, speaking figuratively, no matter how painful the breaking news. The flexible genius of stage-development philosophy is partly that it keeps pointing to how people grow.

Jost et al. give a list of needs of a rigid, authority-stuck personality.

"Mental rigidity and closed-mindedness, including (a) increased dogmatism, and intolerance of ambiguity, (b) decreased cognitive complexity, (c) decreased openness to experience, (d) uncertainty avoidance, (e) personal needs for

[4] Jost, John, Kruglanski, Arie, Glaser, Jack, and Sulloway, Frank, "Political Conservatism as motivated Social Cognition," *Psychological Bulletin*, American Psychological Association, May 2003, Vol. 129, No. 3, 339-375. Please also see page 21 of the 59-page presentation of this essay on the internet at http://www.berkeley.edu/news/media/releases/2003/07/22.

order and structure, and (f) need for cognitive closure; (2)
lowered self-esteem; (3) fear, anger, and aggression; (4) pes-
simism, disgust, and contempt; (5) loss prevention; (6) fear
of death; (7) threat arising from social and economic deprivation; and (8) threat to stability of the social system. We
have argued that these motives are in fact related to one
another psychologically…"[5]

The question to consider, in addition to the psychologists' list
of needs of rigid personalities above, is once such needy personalities get real power, as throughout history they can be seen to get,
and they wield their power over others, what do they champ
about? What do they do when they feel threatened?

5. People brave enough to have built consciences of their own.
Thinking for oneself, being a whole human being, means taking one's own sense of fairness and unfairness seriously. When
Jesus was so sharp-spoken with his parents (at age 12) ("Wist ye
not that I must be about my Father's business?") he had jumped
very far out from stages 2, 3, and 4. Serving God—any god—
instead of just whoever your natural parents and fellow townspeo-
ple are is very, very stage 5 and 6.[6] Serving principles instead of
stated specific groups like one's tribe or one's classmates or one's
church or one's own country is a mark of being a *principled person* in stage 5. Being a critical thinker is a stage 5 quality.

6. Living conscious of and with respect for the universe.
In stage 6 one's horizon has widened and widened and
widened and widened to include all humanity and creatures and

[5] Jost, et al. Cited above
[6] One need not have any religious beliefs at all in moral development. The last half-century has
produced a plethora of studies made by ethicists and sociologists that strongly suggest that
belief systems are non-correlative to altruism or moral compunction. In fact, notably rigid belief
systems often accompany a personal philosophy of us good, them bad, to put it bluntly. We use
Jesus as an example here absolutely not by way of Christian witness at all but because he was
the most resolute abider by his own individual conscience that we know of. In his time everyone was talking about obeying rules and not getting into trouble with the occupying army and
having a right to inherit and having the right to just live your own life to your own comfort and
suddenly here is this man talking about love beyond one's group. He didn't go to college and
read Socrates and Rawls and Wittgenstein and Spinoza. It would be ridiculous not to pay attention to what such an original person has to say.

the air and the water, and for some people of really elegant character, not just our planet but other Milky Way entities and beyond. An interesting, classic side-characteristic of stage 6 thinkers is that they know they can't even begin to be pure like Boy or Girl Scouts. They know that every minute we step on or carve up and eat up something that would have much preferred to live out its life. A stage 6 person does very little self-congratulation.

A final note on the stages: Unfortunately both stages 5 and 6 require some education. One needs to have some sense of the *others* out there who need our respect and some modicum of mercy in order to survive. If we've never heard of them we can't begin to *feel* for them. This makes the unmistakable atrophe of funding for public schooling especially horrible.

Two courageous, early
stage-development thinkers

Friedrich Schiller[1]

1. A natural stage. People start at the natural, thoroughly practical stage. If a viper sees a young chicken wander into its lair, what does it do? What's natural.
2. A beauty-loving stage. Some people, privileged with some education or chance to think, decide they could make their own lives to be beautiful. They hunt out beauty. They learn to do beautiful work. They become *aesthetic*.
3. An ethical stage. A few, very few people develop a hatred of injustice. They agree that beauty is nice and all, but so long as there are cruelty and injustice they devote some of their otherwise comfortable thoughts and life pounding away against such cruelty and injustice. These people have become *ethical*. (Most people don't bother with it.)

George Orwell[2]

1. One wants to write and will sell one's soul a thousand ways in order to get published. (The internet is amazingly full of such folks' shouting.)
2. One gets a taste for writing *beautifully*. Orwell was at Eton where he learned all sorts of elaborate versification. He learned to write very easily and quickly and beautifully—his work of that period being, in his own words, "mostly humbug."
3. A journalist's sort of stage: one looks around and sees there are corners of human activity not yet written up. People should *know* about that stuff. So you do research, and write up whatever odd truths catch your eye.
4. One suddenly notices injustices and hates them with a full heart. In this fourth stage of his own growth, Orwell did the work we honor him for.

---

[1] From *On the Aesthetic Education of Man*, trans and intro. by Wilkinson and Willoughby, Oxford University Press, © 1967 and 1982.
[2] This particular *writers'* development scheme appears in George Orwell's essay, "Why I Write."

"All Humankind...,"

...All human kind,
women and men,
hungry,
hungry beyond the hunger
for food, for justice,
pick themselves up and stumble on
for this: to transcend barriers, longing
for absolution each of each by each,
luxurious unlearning
of lies and fears,
for joy, that throws down the reins
on the neck of
the divine animal
who carries us through the world.

—Denise Levertov

The final stanza of the poem "Modulations"
from *Life in the Forest*, 1978, New York: New Directions.

Mini-Reviews of Two Neurologists
Gerald M. Edelman and Antonio Damasio[1]

Gerald M. Edelman:

"The brain might be said to be in touch more with itself than with anything else."[2]

One of the blessings of our 21st-century culture is the charm and innovation of literature from neuroscience. Scholars in liberal arts fields tend to look to literature and occasionally history for charm in style. We keep being surprised by how well scientists write and how philosophically they think—Lewis Thomas and Richard Selzer from the field of medicine come to mind. The latest surprise is the beauty of neuroscientists' writing, not to mention the innovation in their hypotheses of the last 20 years. Edelman's description of re-entry in the human cortex is exciting and helpful reading for those in literature as well as for those in the helping professions. Ideally, his work should be taken seriously by graduate schools of political science. Schools made use of by the Department of State, however, are characteristically slow to see the reality of modern psychological dynamics. Not only is a prophet not a prophet in his own land, a prophet is not a prophet in his own time, so to speak.

What we suggest is that readers read our chapter on re-entry theory, then make sure to read an original source, *Wider than the Sky* by Edelman, and then read the passages of Wordsworth cited in the Very Small Bibliography. It is marvelous that intuition in Wordsworth led him to an idea of the very brain process now being looked at so respectfully by Dr. Edelman and other neurologists.

---

[1] Please see, in A Very Small Bibliography to Introduce People to Some Up-to-date Neurological Thinking, a few works by Edelman and Damasio, respectively, those listed being books we have read. Both of these scientists have written much more.
[2] Edelman, in *Bright Air, Brilliant Fire*, pp. 18-19.

Antonio Damasio:

If Socrates felt strongly about the virtue of "the life examined" versus the life unexamined, Damasio is even more enthusiastic. Laypeople don't expect a neurosurgeon to express gratitude for what he studies. That is, our mindless expectation is that a scientist always takes care to present his hypotheses and documented findings in a deadbeat voice. Not so with Damasio.

"It is the two gifts combined, consciousness and memory, along with their abundance, that results in the human drama and confers upon that drama a tragic status, then and now."[3]

The author adds "Leading a life examined also brings a privilege and not just a curse. From this perspective, any project for human salvation—any project capable of turning a life examined into a life contented—must include ways to resist the anguish conjured up by suffering and death, cancel it, and substitute joy instead."

Following this Damasio suggests we work at building ourselves a philosophy of whatever particular joys we can fetch to mind because joy and its "related affects" are "more conducive to health and the creative flourishing of our beings." This latter insight is not new to immunologists or social workers or psychologists—but here is what is surprising and beautiful—it is Damasio talking about free will and using psychological muscle (our wording) in order to bear in mind how terrific the universe is. Damasio: "If we do not exist under oppression or in famine and yet cannot convince ourselves how lucky we are to be alive, perhaps we are not trying hard enough."[4]

That's a rouser. It is a rouser to have a neurologist advising in favor of psychological exertion and, however lightly, to scold a little about psychological sloth.

---

[3] Damasio, in *Looking for Spinoza: Joy, Sorrow and the Feeling Brain.* Please see the full reference in A Very Small Bibliography.
[4] Damasio, in *Looking for Spinoza*, pp. 269-271.

Passages from Douglas LaBier

Douglas LaBier, *Modern Madness: The Hidden Link Between Work and Emotional Conflict.* New York: Simon & Schuster (A Touchstone Book), 1986. Passages taken from the author's Preface and from pp. viii and xiii, and from the body of the text, pages 32, 70, 137, and 221-222.

Dr. LaBier very kindly gave us permission to reprint what we chose. His book is by far the most detailed and sympathetic study of corporate executives in a time when it is easier to demonize corporate executives than really think through their moral dilemma. If it is true that America looks increasingly ugly to the world as well as to ourselves now, we can't help noticing that the only beneficiaries of our foreign and domestic policies seem to be large corporations. This has to be a significant, if distressing, psychological predicament for up-and-coming or already up-and-holding executives.

We are immensely grateful to have these passages for *Stopping the Gallop to Empire*.

From the Preface to Modern Madness:
"Questions and observations about how people's emotional lives are affected by the culture of work have been in my mind for several years, since the beginning of my career in the early 1970s. At that time, most practitioners I met had no such interest. In fact, they believed that social, political, economic, and historical forces had nothing whatever to do with understanding or treating emotional problems—and that psychoanalysis had no relation to studying social or moral issues." Page viii.

"In the absence of any clear alternative or solutions [to how executives career paths have affected their lives, and what kinds of lives they are leading, in terms of their relationships, goals, and overall vision], I also see growing desperation regarding how people think of adulthood, judging from how it is portrayed in the popular culture of books, television, and movies. There is a growing theme that being adult is not much fun: a wistful experience of resignation to 'realistic' limitations upon creativity, imagination and love..." p. xiii.

"We tend to assume that the attitudes and behavior which are largely shared by others and therefore 'normal,' are unrelated to emotional troubles. The latter, we prefer to think, belong to a special category of people, who cannot 'adjust' as well as us [sic]. Yet there is a range of emotional and value conflicts which are a product of our well-adjusted attitudes. For example, feelings or criticisms about one's career or the values of one's work can be a handicap to successful advancement if one is too aware of them. So one may repress and ignore those feelings— like anger, self-disgust, boredom, or self-betrayal—if they conflict too much with fitting in and moving up." P.32.

"Based on my seven years of study of people who are the new breed of career professionals in our large organization, I find that adaptation to the values, behavior, and mentality best suited for successful career development has a hidden downside that takes the form of a range of conflicts. They may look neurotic, like Diane [a patient of Dr. LaBier's], because people who suffer from this downside can develop psychological problems like anxiety, depression, rebelliousness, chronic indecisiveness, diminished productiveness, dissatisfaction, feelings of guilt, and various unexplained physical ailments. But ultimately we find that these people are within the range of normal mental health." Pp. 70-71.

"The current transformation which has given rise to the New Normalcy also brings with it a new range of conflicts and troubles that are normal to experience. Because normalcy refers to adaptation, and is not necessarily the same as emotional health, it provides a potential springboard into Modern Madness for the new careerist. This is because the unspoken definition of normalcy and successful adjustment in life now coalesces around that which best makes one into a successful careerist. If your attitudes and values conflict with this, you are in trouble. We have seen in previous chapters that some people's 'normalcy' at work camouflages serious problems because the work 'requires' sick and irrational attitudes. When people adapt to that kind of situation, they don't show any overt symptoms on the job. But they suffer deeply, inside. Their Surface Sanity is reinforced by career environment which make their disturbance functional and adaptive to success."

"For others, a range of mild-to-severe emotional problems or value conflicts develop. Not because they are neurotic, but because their work environment is unhealthy or affects their emotional development in a negative way." P. 137.

"Some companies now give sabbaticals to help employees develop perspective on their lives and careers, to 'recharge' and renew creative energy. Similarly, some organizations, like IBM, have developed the concept of an alternative career path for employees who do not want to move up in management. IBM calls the position an IBM fellow. Outside of the work itself, companies, particularly in high-tech areas which tend to attract the new-breed careerist, offer adjunct health- and recreation-oriented benefits like recreation centers, tennis courts, and swimming pools. Also, increasing numbers of resorts and fitness centers are sponsoring escapes called mental-health breaks, which provided information about stress management, balancing roles and career choices, and women's issues. They focus on ways to cope with stress and set new goals. They encourage reflection about one's values, relationships, career orientation, and exploration of creative and more fulfilling alternatives. Many corporations also offer lunch-hour diversions, such as exercise classes, dance classes, and courses or lectures by college professors. Such extra-career offerings also include efforts by companies to support greater overall interest in health and disease prevention. The assumption is that the expense of such programs pays off in the long run by reducing costs of absenteeism and treatment of disease. Typical programs involve a mixture of exercise, nutritional information, and stress-management education. There is implicit recognition in such programs that the healthy balance for the modern careerist consists of involvement in non-career competencies and sources of stimulation, as we saw earlier in this chapter. The programs support reexamining one's priorities regarding career, family, friendships, and outside activities."

"Based on my work with organizations, I am critical of the usefulness of such programs...

"...these programs are also limited by the 'Big Brother' context in which they exist. Many troubled careerists have told me that they would never talk to the employee-assistance counselor about their conflicts, for fear that it would be used against them. They realize that the counselor or company psychiatrist works for the organization, after all, which compromises the objectivity of the practitioner and limits confidentiality. Moreover, the career professional often questions, rightly or wrongly, the competence of counselors or psychiatrists who work in these settings to begin with. And the programs of help for troubled employees are also marred by an image problem: they are perceived by managerial and professional workers as being primarily for lower-level workers." Pp. 221-222.

Memoir—As the Writing on the Wall

By Carol Bly

Memoir is far the most inviting reading. In grade school we ground out "How Our Family Celebrates Thanksgiving" and "What I Did Over Summer Vacation" so we know the drill. After that, most of us quit writing memoir. It's all changed now.

Yet thousands and thousands of Americans are crowding into graduate writing programs, or into the catchy, comparatively democratic, higher-degree programs like the Master of Liberal Studies and Personal Enrichment Programs. Whatever the program, these Americans want "a writing emphasis" and the writing that most of them mean to emphasize is personal memoir.

Why this 1980s, 1990s, and now 21st century hankering to write up one's own life?—to write it no matter how short our life, and no matter how ordinary? Memoir writers these days don't have to be notables. They aren't Albert Speer or Robert McNamara for whom, given their education and privilege, we readers have many questions.

Considering how powerless most of them are, memoirists confidently expect us to read their books. First-rate historical society presses like the sizable Minnesota Historical Society Press and first-rate university presses and New York publishers of long standing and the trusty midsize presses like Milkweed Editions and Holy Cow! Press are all enthusiastically and successfully publishing memoir by unknown people—a lot of it. Some of these books are wonderfully humorous or philosophical, but clearly a serious reason their authors write and we readers read them is we want to get at something that bothers us about present-day culture. Life in 2001 is anxious. Scientists' forecasts for the planet are not cheerful. Perhaps we are casting about for help, looking backwards. We have been told to look for our own roots. What is equally useful is looking at other people's roots.

We readers want to trust the memoirists not to lie. We hope they haven't "conflated" events or made a "composite" character by boiling together the real aunt and the appalling but witty two cousins. We hope the authors haven't fabricated conversations because they can't remember the real ones. We are looking for serious evidence: how do human beings behave—both conventional human beings and those who can think for themselves? Narrowing the focus, which ways that ordinary people behave make the world stay the way it is, and which ways do some people behave that might be models for us—in case we got up a class action against hopelessness?

You would think that graduate-school writing teachers must feel some disappointment at such an influx of aspiring memoirists, so many of whom don't care two cents' worth for belles lettres: how can they expect ever to learn to write beautifully like Cheri Register[1] or Bill Holm[2] or Solange De Santis[3] or the late Paul Gruchow[4] if they won't study the excellent writing? Ethically grownup professors, however, have a sense of "what winds are walking overhead," as Adrienne Rich wrote about the atom bomb a half-century ago:[5] they feel a moral climate change nearly upon them. They are amenable to dreadful writing. When times are frightening, literature needs deep-thinking, content-based nonfiction, not gorgeous aesthetics. If these cultural or moral historians happen to be gorgeous writers as well, that is welcome icing.

I take memoir-writing to be a life-saving response to the coarse culture we live in. For example, the American workplace heaves and sags with its lying and cheating at even the highest levels. Even comparatively nice corporations hire attorneys to help them evade ecological responsibilities. This is nervous-making stuff, and nervous-making stuff has critical mass in our time. A side-effect: our graduate schools are curiously peopled with folk who hope the MFA will let them get a living outside the corporate setting.

And why is there is so much more writing and reading of

[1] Cheri Register, *Packinghouse Daughter.* St Paul: Minnesota Historical Society Press, ©2000.
[2] Bill Holm, *Eccentric Islands: Travels Real and Imaginary.* Minneapolis: Milkweed Editions, ©2000
[3] Solange De Santis, *Life on the Line: One Woman's Tale of Work, Sweat, and Survival.* New York: Doubleday (A division of Random House)
[4] Paul Gruchow, especially *Grass Roots.* Minneapolis: Milkweed Editions, ©1995.
[5] Adrienne Rich, "A Final Sun," poem in the Wesleyan University Press Younger Poets' Series, 1950.

memoir than of poetry or short fiction? [Of course people still write poems and stories, but not by the tens of thousands the way they take on memoir.]

First, most intelligent nonliterary thinkers secretly dislike poetry, even though poetry is very much like memoir. Most bad poetry is memoir, in fact—bad memoir. Poems lie so scanty on the page, though, like personal memoir with the juicy parts left out. It often poses as surreal even when it isn't. In any case, ordinary intelligent people really hate surrealistic remarks. If in truth

a Tucson alley cat bears the ghost of Alcuin
into the American desert

they don't really want to think about it. To a genuine intellectual who isn't literary the very playfulness of poetry can be infuriating (as even Marianne Moore said in her funny way).

Ordinary readers don't cotton to the short story form either. If D.H Lawrence had been doing something practical, like exposing British upper-middle class track betting patterns, well then!—curiously enough, almost everyone is willing to read sociological anecdote—but in "The Rocking-Horse Winner" Lawrence is so annoyingly worked up about something never said straight out. We can feel him, his mind akimbo as always, jabbing at us, greedy to tell us off about something, pointing up some moral failing, and all the time wanting us to heed him more than we want to.

Poets and short story writers are always wanting us to heed them and we are sick of it. We have civil affairs to think about and a dark global future to think about. We constantly have to make ourselves face some scary likelihoods for our planet. When people feel this serious, the literary mentality strikes us like what Scott Russell Sanders said of human beings generally— constantly speaking as though they understood God but really seeing him only by dim light of a tricky mind.[6]

So memoir yes, poems and tricky fiction, no.

I believe that memoir is the perfect medium for now, even

---

[6] Scott Russell Sanders, in *The Hudson Review*.

for the most literary of us. Here is why. Human life on earth changed in August, 1945. Giambattista Vico, not Thucydides, had the right logic about history. Vico said that history is not cyclical but like a spiral. You never get back to the same place where you'd once been, though you can see down to it through the spiraling. Psychologists tend to comfort people with their singsong "the more it changes the more it stays the same" but that is not only not true, but a distinctly harmful kind of poultice. If we don't recognize how *changed* we are after huge events we won't exert our conscious will to respond with new, needed psychological strengths. Let me use 1945 as a cut-off date, because it brought about the first of the *four terrors we live with now.*

Since 1945 we cannot un-know that nuclear fission kills its intended victims and all life nearby. Then, something called half-life sickens the animals and plants (and us) for tens of thousands of years. We are afraid of this.

Three other new fears have come to our attention since 1945. We can't unknow any of them.

1. The world has radioactivity. Tribal groups of us, one military command or another, use it whenever they want to (most recently in nuclear-tipped artillery in Bosnia and Kosovo). We are afraid of this.

2. Our species has so overpopulated the earth in the last 12,000 years that we are wiping out the large mammals, the small mammals, the fish, and the plant life. We are afraid of this.

3. The globe itself is warming up and *it is our fault.* It is not just part of cyclical climatic pattern. We are seriously afraid for our poor sweating, irreplaceable planet, the only planet we love.

4. And scariest of all, it is not retro kings who do the day's evil, but particular *tribal groups* of us. Some tribal groups hire skilful attorneys to fight off environmentalism. Other tribal groups stunt the cognitive potential of children and we can't stop them from sponsoring the TV programs full of violence and unloving sex. We are afraid of tribal groups.

We can read and write memoirs keeping our eyes open for two kinds of evidence—evidence of how ordinary people's everyday normal behavior may be *enabling* specific tribal groups to do their bad work, and second, evidence of unusual behavior that might *disenable* tribal groups. Meanwhile, brain scientists of the 1990s, of whom general readers and English professors so far take little note, tell us that *all* of homo sapiens have the potential to be history keepers, equipped to develop and even refine electrical places (circuitry) in the brain that let us categorize and record as history our scary and joyful feelings. The brain of everyone in the species, not just of conditioned intellectuals, would like to make connections.

We could teach memoirs to little kids. Look, we could say, the kids of Paul Gruchow's family talked their mother into quitting baking whole-grain bread so they could eat junk commercial white[7]. It was a choice. Memoirs are anecdotal documentation of many weak-minded and strong-minded choices people make. Gruchow actually *lists* ways to oppose the mediocre.

Opposing the mediocre tribe—that's a matter of choice. Freya Manfred, in a very funny deathbed scene, describes how her dying father decided to mentor a rabbit-brained chaplain who visited him in hospital. A rabbit shouldn't go as spiritual counselor to a cobra's bedside but this one did. The chaplain said that she guessed she hadn't read much literature, now he asked. No Catholic theology either, she guessed, though she was a catholic, and no philosophy.[8] Fred urged her to take them all on—literature, theological traditions, philosophy—by way of enrichment. But *not reading* had been her choice, just as *torturing chaplains* was Fred's choice. And we readers get a choice. We can listen to a smart dying man or not.

Memoirs of ordinary life, better than any other genre, show up false cultural generalizations for what they are—false. Here are two from recent books.

The first is political timidity, passed off in the midwest as "stoicism." Nothing to do with Marcus Aurelius, the word is used

---

[7] Gruchow, pp 45-46
[8] Freya Manfred, *A Daughter Remembers: A Literary Memoir.* St Paul: Minnesota Historical Society Press, © 1999, 119f

to mean *unexpressive, even nonreactive under stress.* Farmers are especially prone to it. Being uncomplaining about the weather is twice as manly as whining. But being unexpressive about fla-grant injustice committed by human beings is moral passivity. It is virtual aid and comfort to the enemy. We should give up affectionately kidding midwest farmers for being stoical.

The Minnesota Historical Society Press's Midwest Reflections series are a rich jumble of stoical horror stories. Yet farmers want to be attractive people just as Kathleen Ridder[9] tells us that rich but psychologically abused wives want to be attractive peo-ple. Farmers traditionally put up with exorbitantly cruel sales-styles in lenders and machinery salesmen. Hoffbeck records what farmers endure from those who sell them the huge haylage silos.[10] Ten years ago Deanna Hunter put together a treasure of twenty-six short farm memoirs: documenting exactly how lend-ing agencies and agrosales people bully the farmer.[11] P.C.A. lenders and others jeer at farmers who hesitate to go deeply into debt for huge machinery: the sales people ask, you want to be just a sodbuster or do you want to be an agrobusinessman? Farmers don't jeer back. Robert Amerson tells us that a fieldhand who had been elaborately cheated commented only that "it takes all kinds."[12] Clearly his culture said: philosophical resigna-tion is the good thing, not active, practical protest. In her first-rate stalwart farm memoir[13] Marjorie Douglas describes how indignant she felt that her hard-working husband's ideas for improving the farm program were again and again dismissed summarily by his egocentric father. But the husband said, "'Don't let it bother you. That's just the way he is.'"

The four great terrors of our time since1945 are not our only anxieties, because flesh is still heir to all the griefs Shakespeare

[9] Kathleen Ridder, *Shaping my Feminist Life: A Memoir*, with a Foreword by Jill Ker Conway. St Paul: Minnesota Historical Society Press, ©1998.

[10] Steven R. Hoffbeck, *The Haymakers: A Chronicle of Five Farm Families.* St Paul: Minnesota Historical Society Press, ©2000, 156f.

[11] Deanna Hunter, *Breaking Hard Ground: Stories of the Minnesota Farm Advocates.* Duluth: Holy Cow! Press, ©1990

[12] Robert Amerson, *From the Hidewood: Memories of a Dakota neighborhood.* St Paul: Minnesota Historical Society Press, ©1996, page 177

[13] Marjorie Myers Douglas, *Eggs in the Coffee, Sheep in the Corn.* St Paul: Minnesota Historical Society Press, © 1994, page 44.

noticed—the classical ordinary slings and arrows and contumely of human life. Perhaps we memoir readers and writers and teachers should make two separate lists—one of behaviors to protest—the other of things simply to endure—so we can practice discerning the difference between those lists?

Memoirs scotch the idea that jeering is done only by thugs to control those who have stumbled into their power. We are not surprised that Whites jeered at and beat Native American kids for speaking Ojibwe in the old Indian boarding schools. They not only beat Indian kids but the teaching staff actually jeered at them in the Owatonna State School.[14] That kind of jeering is no longer all right and no one is neutral about it.

What many of us do not understand, however, is how scorn and jeering work among the rich. Exactly how do they work? What actual phrases get used? The rich person's style of jeering is mannerly, often affectionate irony. Affectionate irony—anywhere else called "just kidding"—all on its own has made rich women endure unbelievable disrespect from their own genial, affectionate acquaintance. Kathleen Ridder is the only memoirist I know who is cheerfully upfront about being very rich and a Roman Catholic and a Republican and withal a feminist. From the point of view of cultural history, she is a Brearley and Smith grad. She gives us cultural history in anecdotes of how rich people help one another, but also in how the stronger of them control the less strong. The story is the more interesting because Ridder has been a raiser of serious money for good causes, something men of her class quite naturally network to do, but women only recently. When women first went after decent-sized (versus bakesale priced) donation amounts, Ridder tells us males dropped snide references to "rich women downtown."[15]

American literature is sadly short of serious memoirs by the rich. I expect that is because most cultural life happens in living-

[14] Two books of memoir in the Minnesota Historical Society Press's Native Voices Series are *Living our Language: Ojibe Tales and History*, edited by Anton Treuer, ©2001 and J. Peter Razor's *While the Locust Slept*, ©2001. Treuer and Razor report on the traditional, nearly unbelievable bullying of Native American children by white adults.
[15] Kathleen Ridder C., *Shaping my Feminist Life: A memoir*, with a Foreword by Jill Ker Conway. St Paul: Minnesota Historical Society Press, ©1998, 199.

rooms Not much is known about how the rich develop their feelings, such as exactly how they feel entitled, how they just as genuinely feel noblesse oblige—yet at the same time want the poor kept far off-location. They want the tiresome, humorless middle class out of their living rooms, too.

Rich women write few memoirs. Too bad, because the very rich are so influential in three of the four major anxieties of our time (radioactive weaponry, global warming, and TV programming) we have questions for them, interesting, psychological questions, too: what makes them comply with what comes down? For those who didn't comply, what gave them the spunk to hold out? And at what sacrifice—did someone, for all his promises, forget to write your daughter the needed recco to Groton because you spoke out against some civic cruelty or other?

History is written by the noisy triumphant, the theme being, "Despite what we were up against, here is how I made it happen." The new memoirs are a relief, coming as they do from the little as well as the great, the thoughtful, the confused, some from people who have been perfect terrors. Barbara Tuchman and Virginia Woolf, who made their psychological assays from personal documents, would have snatched up these new memoirs. They were always asking, what makes someone be sensible or fair in a crisis? Or, what unconscious or conscious egoism makes someone cause millions to suffer?

Tuchman and Woolf would have read today's memoirs the way some of us secretly do. If we are in English departments, we have to pretend that only the literary tech of them or the aesthetic settings of them were of interest. "O yes," we say aloud, because aestheticism is the harbor flag on the shiniest liners , "I *am* reading that—talk about beautiful writing!"—when all the while we are really looking and looking to find out what in the world is going on! How can our species sleep at night?

Index

Carol Bly and Cynthia Loveland are the proprietors of Bly & Loveland Press (*Three Readings for Republicans and Democrats*). Carol Bly's most recent books are *Changing the Bully who Rules the World*, 1996, *My Lord Bag of Rice*, 2000, and *Beyond the Writers' Workshop: New Ways to Write Creative Nonfiction*, 2001. Cynthia Loveland, MSW, ACSW, a School Social Worker for the St. Paul, Minnesota, schools, has served as chair of the Pamphlet Advocacy Committee of the Minnesota School Social Workers' Association (MSSWA) and on the Board of the Minnesota Chapter of the National Association of Social Workers (NASW).